I CH

PLAIN & SIMPLE

I CHING

PLAIN & SIMPLE

KIM FARNELL

THE ONLY BOOK YOU'LL EVER NEED

HAMPTON ROADS

Cover design by Jim Warner
Interior design by Kathryn Sky-Peck
Image on facing page: Fu Hsi recording the eight trigrams
(artwork from the China Story Project, *www.TheChinaStory.org*)

Hampton Roads Publishing Company, Inc.
Charlottesville, VA 22906
Distributed by Red Wheel/Weiser, LLC
www.redwheelweiser.com
Sign up for our newsletter and special offers by going to
www.redwheelweiser.com/newsletter/

ISBN: 978-1-57174-779-2

Library of Congress Control Number: 2016959342

Printed in Canada
MAR

10 9 8 7 6 5 4 3 2 1

Contents

What Is the I Ching?

The words *I Ching* (usually pronounced *EE Ching* or *YEE Ching*) translate into English as "The Book of Changes."

The I Ching may be the oldest book in existence. Dating back to 1000 BC, it is an ancient divination text that has evolved over many centuries, later including a mix of Taoist and Confucian philosophy. The philosophy behind the I Ching is that nothing is static and that everything changes over time, so our task is to adjust to the ebb and flow of changing circumstances.

I Ching Plain and Simple is not a translation of the I Ching. It is a book that explains the divinatory system of the I Ching and provides interpretations for each of the hexagrams in clear, modern language. The I Ching can help us to make decisions that logic alone can't handle, therefore reducing the stress that decision making can cause. It enables us to manage sensitive relationships more successfully, to develop better timing and to tap into our creative insight and intuitive power.

Consulting the I Ching is different from using runes or tarot cards because its main task is not to tell the future as much as to make a situation more clear and to offer useful advice. It relies on the fact that achieving good fortune and avoiding misfortune depends on the choices that we make. When we consult the I Ching, we do not sit back and passively accept our destiny but actively create our own fortune. If our actions are in keeping with the advice of the I Ching, our fortune will be good. If our actions are out of harmony with the counsel or if we refuse to act when action is called for, then things won't go as smoothly. Having said that, the I Ching often does offer guidance about the future.

Bodhidharma consulting the I Ching (artwork from the China Story Project, www.TheChinaStory.org)

Origins of I Ching

It is likely that the I Ching is the oldest form of divination on earth, as its origins reach back eight thousand years or so to the end of the Ice Age! The mythology of the origins of the I Ching includes the tale of Fu Hsi, the first emperor of China (3rd millennium BC). The story tells us that Fu Hsi was sitting on the bank of the Yellow River when he saw a turtle emerge from the water. He paid close attention because he knew that all true wisdom came from observing nature. In his observation he noticed eight markings on the turtle's shell; these became the original eight trigrams of the I Ching.

Out of this came the practice of tortoise shell and ox shoulder-bone divination. A red-hot poker was applied to ox bones, and wise men or "priests" deduced their meaning from the random pattern of cracks that appeared. Ancient Chinese soothsayers looked for portents in the cracks of tortoise shells, which were heated over a fire and then dowsed with water. The

Tortoise shell with divination inscription from the Shang dynasty, dating to the reign of King Wu Ding, circa 1200 BC. National Museum of China

geometric patterns made by the resulting cracks were then studied and analyzed. A secondary possible source of I Ching wisdom came from reading the lines that one can see on the flanks of an ancient type of northern Chinese horse. Whatever the origins, the patterns of cracks inspired a systematic method that has developed over the centuries into today's I Ching. This comes about via reading a three-line design that is called a trigram and a six-line design that is composed of two trigrams and which is called a hexagram.

The earliest appearance of a translation of the I Ching in the West was a Latin translation made in the 1730s by a Jesuit missionary. The most influential translation into a modern Western language was made by Richard Wilhelm in 1923. Since then it has been translated numerous times and has grown in popularity in the West until the present time.

Yin and Yang and the I Ching

1

Yin and yang are mutually dependent opposites. Looking at the world in terms of yin and yang gives one a real sense of how fluid the universe is, and no matter how you are feeling today, things are bound to change. As the Chinese say, you can never step into the same river twice. Yin originally meant "shady, secret, dark, lunar, mysterious and cold" like the shaded, north side of a mountain. Yang meant "clear, bright, solar and hot" like the lighted south side of a mountain. From these basic opposites, a complete system of opposites developed. Yin represents everything about the world that is dark, hidden, passive, receptive, yielding, cool, soft and feminine. Yang represents everything about the world that is illuminated, evident, active, aggressive, controlling, hot, hard and masculine.

Everything can be identified as either yin or yang. Earth is the ultimate yin object and heaven is the ultimate yang object. Although yin is feminine and yang masculine, most things (and people) are a mixture of the two. The familiar diagram of yin and yang flowing into each other shows the yin side with a yang dot within it and vice versa. This symbolizes the fact that each force contains the seed of the other and that under certain circumstances they can actually become the other.

Yin and Yang Characteristics

	Yin	Yang
Nature	Feminine	Masculine
	Passive	Active
	Broken line	Unbroken line
	Receives	Creates
	Soft	Hard
	Dark	Bright
Symbols	Moon	Sun
	Tiger	Dragon
	North	South
Color	Black	Red
Numbers	Even	Odd
Chinese character	陰	陽
Original meaning	North side of a hill (away from the sun)	South side of a hill (facing the sun)

Trigrams and Hexagrams

The I Ching contains trigrams and hexagrams. A trigram is composed of three lines, and a hexagram is composed of six lines.

Some of the lines are complete:

Other lines have a small break half way along.

A **trigram** may contain three unbroken lines, three broken ones or a mixture of both. Here is a typical trigram:

Each **hexagram**, which is actually two trigrams that have been placed one above the other, is made up of six lines. A hexagram can have any combination of unbroken or broken lines. Here is a typical example of a mixed hexagram.

There are eight trigrams and 64 hexagrams (eight times eight) in the I Ching. Interestingly, the German philosopher and mathematician Gottfried Wilhelm Leibniz, who invented the binary system later used in computers, derived his inspiration from the I Ching: the binary instructions given to a computer consist of a mixture of ones and zeros, echoing the unbroken and broken lines of the I Ching.

The lines in the hexagrams represent the principles of yang and yin: the unbroken lines represent yang, while the broken ones represent yin. In the West, we are accustomed to writing across a page or by making a list that goes down the page, but in the I Ching, we create the hexagrams by starting at the bottom and working upward.

Casting
the
I Ching

2

The I Ching can't be used to give an overview of the future in the general way that the tarot can; it is designed to give an answer to a specific question. It is worth spending some time defining your question, perhaps noting it down in order to clarify it in your own mind.

Need a Quick Answer?

The full I Ching is extremely complex and its philosophies link to all aspects of life. The I Ching underpins Chinese astrology, Feng Shui, face reading and even Chinese palmistry! Despite the complexities, the point of this book is to make things as plain and simple as possible, so that an absolute beginner can use the system right away.

What if you are at work and you need a quick answer? Use this quick method because it doesn't require any equipment or preparation. Open this book at the pages that show all the hexagrams (pages 18–19) and then focus mentally on your question while drifting your fingers lightly over the page. You don't need to touch the page, just allow your fingers to wander over it until you find one or two hexagrams "drawing" you toward them. Some people will feel a slight change in temperature as though one of the hexagrams heats up slightly, others will just feel drawn to one or two hexagrams for no logical reason.

A variation on this theme is to use a pendulum. The best form of temporary pendulum is a necklace, especially one that has a pendant dangling on it. The only thing to mention is that this must be your own necklace and not one that you have borrowed from a friend or you might get your friend's reading instead of yours!

If you are using this quick and easy method, find your hexagram then skip to chapter 6, "Quick Interpretations" to find your answer.

To be honest, these quick methods are not the correct way to consult the I Ching, as preparing to read this ancient text is in itself a form of meditation that takes you from the workaday world and puts you in the right frame of mind to accept the advice this ancient text provides.

Casting

The simplest form of casting is to use three coins. You can buy copies of ancient Chinese coins in a gift shop and keep these for your I Ching readings, or you can ask your bank to give you three shiny new coins. It is best to use three coins of the same denomination, as they will be the same size and weight. If you use Chinese coins, you will need to choose which side will represent "heads" to you and which will be "tails."

Whatever coins you use, keep them aside and use them specifically for your I Ching readings. The Chinese say that anything that you use for divination creates a link with the gods so keep your tools above head height, as this is closer to the gods. This also keeps them out of harm's way. It is nice to give your readings a touch of ceremony, so you might want to use a decorative cloth and keep it with your coins.

Now practice for a while. Throw your three coins gently onto your special cloth and see how they fall. They may all land the same way up or two will land one way up and the third will land the other way. If the majority of coins land as heads, this will be yang, but if the majority are tails, this will be yin.

Making a Start

Always have pen and paper on hand so that you can note the outcomes of your castings. Throw the coins gently while thinking of your question and then leave your coins on the table for a while. If the majority of coins are yang (heads) draw a straight line.

▬▬▬▬▬▬▬▬▬▬▬▬▬

If the majority of the coins are yin (tails) draw a line with a break in it.

▬▬▬   ▬▬▬

If you have thrown *three* heads or *three* tails draw a little cross in the middle of your line.

▬▬▬✗▬▬▬

▬▬ X ▬▬

This special line is called a "changing line," and its importance will be discussed later.

After you have drawn your first line, pick up and throw your coins again, but draw your second line *above* the first. Then do the same again, drawing each new line above the last, until you have six lines.

Your result will look something like the example below.

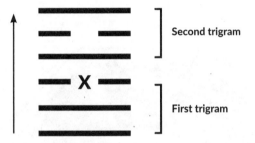

Now you can read on to discover what your hexagram means. Don't forget that all hexagrams are made up from two trigrams, and each trigram has information to offer in addition to the information contained in the whole hexagram. The lower three lines contain the first trigram and the upper three contain the second trigram.

Finding Your Hexagrams

3

ow that you have drawn your lines, look at your illustration and compare it to the table below to find the hexagram that matches yours. For the time being, ignore any crosses that you may have marked. Finding your hexagram in the chart is a procedure takes a little time and patience but that alone makes it act as a form of meditation that takes you away from the rush and bustle of daily life.

If you're using the quick and easy method, go straight to chapter 6, "Quick Interpretations" to find your plain and simple answer.

The 64 Hexagrams

| 1 | 2 | 3 | 4 | 5 | 6 | 7 | 8 |

| 9 | 10 | 11 | 12 | 13 | 14 | 15 | 16 |

| 17 | 18 | 19 | 20 | 21 | 22 | 23 | 24 |

25 26 27 28 29 30 31 32

33 34 35 36 37 38 39 40

41 42 43 44 45 46 47 48

49 50 51 52 53 54 55 56

57 58 59 60 61 62 63 64

The Lines

Hexagrams With No "Changing" Lines

After six throws of the coins, you will end up with six lines. You will recall from the discussion on page 14, when you throw three of a kind—all heads or all tails—the result will be a "changing" line. If all six of the lines in your hexagram were arrived at by throwing coins where two were of one kind and one was of the other kind, you will not draw a little cross on any of the lines, which means none will be "changing" lines.

All you need to do now is to find the hexagram in the illustration, and look it up in the interpretation section in this book (chapter 5, "Interpreting the Hexagrams"). A hexagram that has no changing lines suggests that your current situation or problem is almost at an end.

Each hexagram comprises two trigrams. The lower trigram indicates your own actions, while the upper trigram refers to the actions of others. The trigrams also offer further information about direction, time of the year, and so on, as you will see in chapter 4, "The Trigrams."

Hexagrams With Changing Lines

If one or more of the lines have been created as the result of a three-of-a-kind throw—three heads (yang) or three tails (yin)—you must mark the lines or lines with a small cross in the middle.

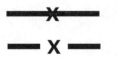

three heads

three tails

This shows that the situation you asked about in your question is ongoing, and your reading will show whether you have to live with it, you can improve it, or you should walk away from it if you can. In the case of a hexagram that contains one or more changing lines, after you have read the interpretation for the hexagram, you must read the interpretation for any of the lines marked with a cross.

The Changes in Action

Once you have read the information and the information on each of the changing lines, alter the marked lines so that an unbroken yang lines becomes a broken yin lines and vice versa.

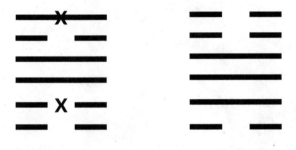

| Original hexagram | Changed hexagram |

As you can see, the marked lines have now changed from yang to yin or vice versa and you now have a new hexagram to read. The second hexagram will offer further information on the current situation and its outcome.

The
Trigrams

4

You can pull your hexagrams apart to make two trigrams. As always with the I Ching, you must start with the bottom line and work upward. Draw the lower three lines on a piece of paper and mark this "inner trigram." Then draw the upper three lines and mark this "outer trigram."

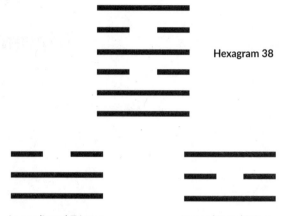

Hexagram 38

Lower (Inner) Trigram   Upper (Outer) Trigram

There are eight possible trigram patterns. In addition to the interpretation you will find for each hexagram, you will discover that there are many ideas that are linked to each trigram, in much the same way that many different things are linked to the signs of the zodiac in Western astrology. Here is a list of a few basic topics that might help you to make more of your I Ching reading.

For instance, a particular family member (father, mother, sister) might be involved in your reading. If family figures don't apply in your life, the person might be similar in some way to a parent figure, brother or sister figure, and so on. For example, your boss might be represented by a parent figure and a colleague or friend could be symbolized by a brother or sister figure.

A certain direction may be important to you, such as north, south, northeast and so on. Or perhaps a time of the year or a time of day may be significant. A color might have some significance, as might a number. For instance, the trigram might forecast the color of the front door or the number of the house, the time of day that you enter it and so on.

This chapter will review each of the eight possible trigrams, providing you the keywords and concepts associated with each so you can explore the ideas embedded in your hexagram.

A Recap

- Read your hexagram as a whole.

- If you have marked any lines with a cross, read these.

- Split your hexagram into two trigrams.

- First read the trigram formed by the lower three lines. This signifies the things that *you* want, what is going on in your mind, or the effect of the action that you might take.

- Now read the trigram formed by the upper three lines of the hexagram. This trigram suggests outside influences that may bear on your question.

- Now take the lines that you have marked with a cross (changing lines) and alter them over so that any yang lines are now yin and vice versa. This creates a second hexagram.

- Read the new hexagram and the trigrams that it makes.

The Trigrams in Detail

When a hexagram is formed by a double trigram (that is, the same pattern above as below), the meaning of the hexagram is intensi-fied. This configuration suggests that you need to pay extra heed to the guidance given or the situation that is depicted.

Here are the interpretations for each of the eight trigrams, and their correspondences. The trigrams are always listed in the order that follows.

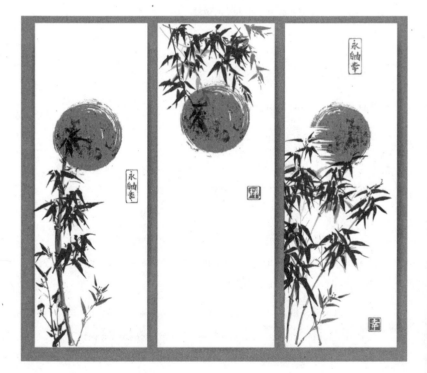

CHIEN

Name	Heaven
Family member	Father
Body parts	Head and mind
Season	Late autumn
Direction	Northwest
Time	Daytime
Motion	Upward
Color	White, gold
Number	Six

This pure yang trigram is one of the two most powerful of all the trigrams. It is entirely masculine and it represents action, drive and energy. Chien represents the power of heaven or the power that is held by the head of a family or organization. It represents authority, power, strength, creativity, logic and courage. Chien suggests a time when you must focus your mind and energies on a particular goal in order to achieve your ambition. While the trigram can symbolize any part of your life, the chances are that this trigram concerns your career, working for an exam or achieving any goal that you have in mind. Chien shows a desire to be in control and to put things in order.

K'UN

Name	Earth
Family member	Mother (also ordinary member of the public)
Body parts	Stomach, abdomen and womb
Season	Late summer
Direction	Southwest
Time	Night
Motion	Downward
Color	Black, dark colors
Number	Two

This entirely feminine trigram is one of the two most important trigrams. The three broken lines of K'un symbolize earth as a support for human life as well as the burial ground for death. The earth is soft and receptive and it can take punishment with a high degree of tolerance. K'un seeks to leave things as they are. Loyalty and practicality combine with inner strength, so that a K'un person is the one who you can turn to in a crisis. The most feminine of the trigrams, K'un represents the attributes of care, nurture and consideration for others. It relates to feelings and emotions as well as intuition. The key ideas associated with K'un are receptivity, endurance, acceptance, patience and docility.

CHEN

Name	Thunder
Family member	Eldest son (or a strong worker, leader, artist or inventor)
Body parts	Foot, throat and voice
Season	Spring
Direction	East
Time	Early morning
Motion	Upward
Color	Yellow
Number	Three

The two broken lines on top convey the image of a lightning strike and the bottom solid line symbolizes elevation. Thus, the image is that of lightning striking the top of a mountain. Chen symbolizes the birth of an idea and the independence and assertion to act on it. Shock tactics can be used to gain effect and it can produce revolutionary results. Chen is associated with regeneration. It represents male arousal and sexuality, fertility, initiative, action and energy.

K'AN

Name	Water
Family member	Middle son (also aggressive young men)
Body parts	Ear, kidneys
Season	Winter
Direction	North
Time	Midnight
Motion	Downward
Color	Blue
Number	One

A solid line between two broken lines symbolizes water. The two broken lines represent riverbanks with a river running between them. The solid line in the middle represents motion, so this creates the image of water flowing in a river. K'an is independent and self-reliant as it believes in doing things for itself. The masculine line in the midst of two feminine lines represents a form of transition or changes that can bring danger.

K'an represents turning points or times when you are not in control of events. Uncertainty, unpredictable times, danger and stress are shown by this trigram. In favorable circumstances, the change can be a challenge; at other times it is something to be feared. It shows hard times and desires that are unlikely to be fulfilled for the time being.

KEN

Name	Mountain
Family member	Youngest son (or priests, monks, prisoners, the infirm, and boys below age sixteen)
Body parts	Hand, spine
Season	Early spring
Direction	Northeast
Time	Just before dawn
Motion	Downward
Color	Violet
Number	Eight

A solid line above two broken lines symbolizes a mountain. The solid line represents height and the bottom two broken lines represent earth as a base. Thus this image is a mountain elevated above the earth. It represents keeping still and holding onto the past to keep things as they were. Ken represents a time of retreat and reflection when spiritual issues take precedence over worldly ones. Earthly concerns can be forgotten while one concentrates on religious or philosophical ideas. It shows a time of silence, isolation and withdrawal. Those represented by this trigram seek seclusion or they may find themselves temporarily secluded, hospitalized or otherwise cut off from life.

SUN

Name	Wind or wood
Family member	Eldest daughter (women up to middle age, travelers, business people)
Body parts	Thigh, upper arm, lungs, and nerves
Season	Early summer
Direction	Southeast
Time	Midmorning
Motion	Downward
Color	Green
Number	Four

The two solid lines above a broken line symbolize wind. The two solid lines represent the sky while the broken line represents earth. The wind is invisible and we can see its existence only by observing the moving treetops. Sun represents evolution, slow growth and gradual change for the better. It represents feminine virtues of endurance, gentle determination, adaptability and fair play.

LI

Name	Fire
Family member	Middle daughter (or young women, craftsmen and artists)
Body parts	Eyes, blood, and heart
Season	Summer
Direction	South
Time	Noon
Motion	Upward
Color	Orange
Number	Nine

A broken line between two solid lines symbolizes fire. The two solid lines show the movement of a fire while the broken line is the unmoving center of the fire. Li represents mutual support, welfare and helping others. It also relates to illumination and inspiration, clarity and knowledge. It represents those who are generous and big hearted.

☱ TUI

Name	Marsh or lake
Family member	Youngest daughter (or girls up to age sixteen, mistresses)
Body parts	Mouth, lips, and tongue
Season	Autumn
Direction	West
Time	Evening or late afternoon
Motion	Upward
Color	Red
Number	Seven

A broken line on top of two solid lines symbolizes a marsh. The top broken line represents water and the bottom two solid lines symbolize the sky. If we look down at a body of water we see the reflected sky below. Tui is inventive, entrepreneurial and always ready to do business. Tui represents the psychic world and it is associated with healing, magic, joy and pleasure. It often refers to women who are fun to be with but who have no power within the family—such as mistresses or friends.

Seasons, Time, and the Trigrams

The trigrams can be quite helpful because each refers to a specific time of year, so it is easy to see how a certain season might be relevant to your question.

Chien	Late autumn
K'un	Late summer
Chen	Spring
K'an	Winter
Ken	Early spring
Sun	Early summer
Li	Summer
Tui	Autumn

The trigrams also relate to specific times of day and to certain times. As usual, the first two trigrams (Chien, heaven and K'un, earth) are the most important and each of these two has three possible meanings.

Chien	Daytime; late evening up to midnight; or one day into the future
K'un	Night; afternoon; or one month into the future
Chen	Early morning
K'an	Midnight
Ken	Just before dawn
Sun	Midmorning
Li	Noon
Tui	Evening or late afternoon

Using the Trigrams

An Example for Someone Who Is Seeking Work

You want a new job and you don't know where to start to look for it. Draw a hexagram that is made up of the trigrams, Li and K'an, with Li at the bottom and K'an above. Li represents south and K'an north, so you should look along a north/south line that runs through your home. What falls along that north-south line? Your kitchen? A computer? A large sunny room with plants? These could all be keys to a possible career choice.

Now take a map of your town or your area and extend the line 20 miles to the north and south. Look along that line and about 20 miles on either side of it. Your new job opportunity will likely be found in that area.

Incidentally, if you cast your coins and draw a hexagram made up of the trigrams Li and K'an, the job might be on the horizon. A young woman might point you in the right direction.

The trigram K'an

The trigram Li

Interpreting the Hexagrams

5

In this chapter, you will find the trigrams that make up each hexagram and the interpretations for each hexagram including all the changing line interpretations. If you haven't read all the instructions, now is the time to go back over the book and read them.

1. CHIEN

CREATIVITY. THE KING

Upper trigram: Chien. Creativity. Heaven.

Lower trigram: Chien. Creativity. Heaven.

The Image

Heaven is supremely powerful, it doesn't get tired, it doesn't suddenly decide to stop being heaven—and there is only one heaven. The doubling of any trigram indicates movement but in the case of Chien, there is in the sense that time always moves on and that we must move now to deal with something before things change.

Interpretation

Made up from two Chien trigrams, Chien is pure yang and the most masculine, fatherly and muscular of the hexagrams. Determination will be needed in order to change and transform a situation. To get what you want, you need to act bravely and confidently. Although obstacles lie ahead, persistence will overcome them. Focus on your goals and go all out for what you want. Initiate new ideas and use your energy wisely. At work, you need to show leadership and strength. In your personal life your loved ones will turn to you for direction. It's important to use your strength wisely without being aggressive or obstinate. This could be the beginning of a new phase in your life.

Chien represents the start of something that is advantageous, correct and firm. It shows benevolence, righteousness, propriety and knowledge. Success will come, and everything depends upon your actively seeking happiness and persevering with what you know to be right. You can bring peace and security through creating order.

Lowest line

Do not act yet. Your talents have not been recognized. Remain true to yourself and wait because the time is not yet ripe.

Second line up

Your ability to bring matters into being is growing. Let your ideas flow and settle into shape. Your seriousness of purpose, reliability and influence make you look good in the eyes of others. Contact those who can help you.

Third line up

All day you are busy and all night your mind is in turmoil. Your creative energy is on the increase. There is much to be done, so when others rest you worry. It is time to turn your back on the past, even though what you did in the past was right. Your influence is growing.

Fourth line up

This is a period of transition. You need to choose between soaring to the heights and playing an important part in the world or withdrawing into solitude to develop yourself. So long as you are true to yourself you will find the best way.

Fifth line up

Seek out people who can help you. Make things, build, create and establish. Your influence is increasing.

Top line

Avoid arrogance. You will regret it if you try to enforce your authority. If you go overboard you will have cause for regret. Pride leads to a fall.

When all the lines are marked for change it means that the whole hexagram is in motion and it will change into the hexagram K'un, which means passivity and receptivity rather than taking action.

2. K'UN

RECEPTIVITY. THE QUEEN

Upper trigram: K'un. Receptivity. Earth.

Lower trigram: K'un. Receptivity. Earth.

The Image

As is the case with heaven, the earth is unchanging, so the doubling of the trigram means that the usual change and movement that occurs when the energies switch back and forth between the trigrams is absent. The earth will never change much—whatever good or harm is done to it. The figure, which is made up of six divided lines, expresses the ideal of subordination and docility. It represents nature in contrast to spirit, earth in contrast to heaven, space as against time and the maternal female rather than the paternal male. There is only one earth, so the doubling of the trigram implies endurance.

Interpretation

Made up from two K'un trigrams, K'un is pure yin and the most feminine and motherly of the hexagrams. This suggests that you need to adjust to circumstances, fit in and not make waves. You are confronted with many conflicting forces. To some extent your future happiness is in the hands of others or else it involves others—so it's important not to think of yourself as alone. However, you still need to maintain your sense of purpose and do what needs to be done. Trying to take the lead can make you go astray—you need guidance at this time.

The feminine virtues of endurance, duty, fitting in and waiting for things to come right are emphasized. You have the power to accept the inevitable. Although times can be confusing, don't worry. You need to go with the flow for a while and trust your intuition. Joining others for concrete purposes will achieve a lot. By yielding and providing what is needed you can open up a new cycle. Accept that some things are hidden from you and don't set up boundaries about what you will or will not do.

Lowest line

Act carefully to establish a base. Things are beginning to solidify.

Second line up

Focus on a single idea. Establish that first, and as long as you are sincere, you will be able to achieve this one aim. Don't try to take on any more than you already have on your plate and don't take on anything new because you have not yet worked out all that needs to be done.

Third line up

You shouldn't bring your part in things to an end because you need to be visible and to have your efforts on show. You can be successful on behalf of others. Send out feelers in new directions and you will make important discoveries.

Fourth line up

What you want is out there waiting for you. Whatever you do will be acceptable, so you will neither be blamed nor praised for your efforts. Think before you act.

Fifth line up

Sticking to what works, avoiding foolish ideas and acting with discretion will bring supreme good fortune.

Top line

Don't let a situation of conflict continue. If you are responsible for the impasse, give in and restore the peace.

When all the lines are marked for change, it is best to persevere and do the right thing.

3. CHUN

DIFFICULTY AT THE BEGINNING

Upper trigram: K'an. The abyss. Water.

Lower trigram: Chen. The arousing. Thunder.

The Image

The image associated with Chun is that of a blade of grass, struggling from the earth and gradually rising above the surface. These first stages of growth symbolize the struggle that marks the start of something new and a time when great changes are made. It brings order out of confusion.

Interpretation

This is the start of a new phase and you don't yet know where it will lead. You don't know the risks you face. You need to strip away old ideas because everything is changing and you must break new ground now. Although things may get off to a slow start they will improve, so you can reach your goals in a slow and steady manner. You have a lot of work to do. Things come at you from all sides but you can find the help that you will need in order to deal with them. Do not act prematurely or alone. You need helpers but you shouldn't just leave them to get on with it, so lend a hand where it is needed. There is a chance of a new relationship. You will make progress by doing what is right and by persisting. Changes should not be lightly made.

Lowest line

You need to establish firm foundations and to take advantage of any help that is offered.

Second line up

Your difficulties pile up. Every time you start something you run into obstacles. You need to make alliances and realize that forces that are beyond your control are at work.

Third line up

If you continue to act in this way you will lose your direction. Don't reject help when it is offered. Be prepared to give up if the situation demands it and avoid doing something you may regret.

Fourth line up

You need to actively seek alliances because this will help.

Fifth line up

Give people what they need and don't impose your ideas on them.

Top line

Why allow this bad situation to continue? It is time to retreat.

When all the lines can change, it means that you must persevere. Stick to your guns and do what is right because then you will benefit.

4. MENG

YOUTH, FOLLY, INEXPERIENCE

Upper trigram: Ken. Keeping still. Mountain.

Lower trigram: K'an. The abyss. Water.

The Image

The image is of a spring welling up at the foot of the mountain and it is considered an image of youth. The water flows out but it doesn't yet know what direction to take. Meng suggests youthful inexperience and ignorance.

Interpretation

You are immature and you may have a clouded view of your problem because you don't really know what you are doing. You need to gain or update skills or obtain an education or qualifications. Take advice and learn slowly. Sometimes you feel confused and need to work through things steadily until you understand them. If you are misunderstood, take the time to explain yourself to others. You may have a one-sided view of things. Don't put on airs and graces but be ready to listen to advice. Treat others kindly and generously. There is nothing wrong with being inexperienced. Seek out someone wiser and more experienced to offer you the advice that you need.

Lowest line

Restrain those who do things wrongly—but don't keep an unnecessarily tight control on yourself. However, you will need to be self-disciplined to avoid making a fool of yourself.

Second line up

You need to take a responsible attitude and to care for things. Be kind to those who know less than you do.

Third line up

Don't be grasping. It does you no good to rely on status symbols or material things, even though you feel that these will give you satisfaction.

Fourth line up

Your isolation distances you from what is real, so you need to correct your thinking. Acting in ignorance will give you cause for regret.

Fifth line up

You get what you want by yielding and by gently working toward your goal. Although you're inexperienced, things turn out well.

Top line

You need to resist the temptation to break the rules or behave violently. Work within your situation rather than fighting it.

5. HSU

WAITING

Upper trigram: K'an. The abyss. Water.

Lower trigram: Chien. Creativity. Heaven.

The Image

This is the image of clouds rising to the heavens. We need nourishment from above but it comes in its own time and we may have to wait. This hexagram shows the clouds in the heavens, giving rain to refresh all that grows and providing us with food and drink. The rain will come in its own time. We cannot make it come; we have to wait for it.

Interpretation

By acting sincerely and waiting for the right moment, you can have the success that you want, but you must first find out what is required. You will not hang around unnecessarily right now because you are certain to reach your goal. You are faced with a problem that needs to be overcome. Weakness and impatience can do nothing. It is only when you have the courage to face things exactly as they are, without self-deception or illusion, that the path to success may be recognized. It is up to you to act on that recognition. Although you may feel that you should act boldly and confront what is wrong in your life, it would be better to wait until you are sure of success. You're not in full control of what is happening. There is danger ahead, so don't plunge into anything. If life is quiet, take a rest and wait for busier times to come. Talk over your ideas with others and listen to their advice. Ambition and advancement are on the way, even if they are not evident yet. This is a time to spread harmony and to do the right thing. Others will admire your accomplishments. Crossing water for business or personal reasons can be beneficial.

Lowest line

You need to wait in the background. It may be hard to do this but perseverance will bring you insight. Maintaining things as they are now will prevent problems in the future.

Second line up

You need to adapt to the small people and to the ideas that others have. Although you may be the victim of gossip things will turn out well in the end.

Third line up

You feel bogged down and unable to move out of harm's way to avoid being hurt. You need to understand how you got into this situation and find a way out of it.

Fourth line up

Although you feel stuck in a disastrous place, you can be saved if you're prepared to listen.

Fifth line up

You need to spend time with others and to eat and drink with them. Be reliable and do what is right and everything will turn out well.

Top line

Three people unexpectedly offer you help that you haven't asked for. If you offer them your respect they will help you out of your present situation.

6. SUNG

CONFLICT

Upper trigram: Chien. Creativity. Heaven.

Lower trigram: K'an. The abyss. Water.

The Image

Heaven and the abyss are pulling you in two opposing directions. Your life is full of contradiction at present.

Interpretation

Although you're probably in the right, this is not a good time to argue or make your point. Try to express yourself without escalating the conflict. It doesn't matter how sincere you are, others will argue with you, and you may have to meet your opponent halfway. Don't be intimidated but avoid petty arguments because there's a good chance you will lose them. Accept criticism or lack of credit for what you've done for now. Don't attempt large undertakings at work or elsewhere—maintaining a steady course is the best option. It is not a good time to try to complete things. Asking for advice is wise. Act cautiously. Relationships are not favorable now as this is not a harmonious time.

Lowest line

Get out of this affair. Say what you need to say and go. This way you will avoid a long and bitter conflict.

Second line up

Don't try to control the situation by arguing. It's best to give way and return to where doors are open for you.

Third line up

Take advantage of the work done by your predecessors. You will accomplish what you have been asked to do but you may not receive credit for it.

Fourth line up

Turn away rather than argue. Submit to fate and an opportunity will come to you.

Fifth line up

Put your case over confidently and expect good results. You can correct what has gone wrong.

Top line

You may be showered with money and credit, but by the end of the morning will lose it three times over. This temporary success will gain you nothing in the end.

7. SHIH

LEADERSHIP

Upper trigram: K'un. Receptivity. Earth.

Lower trigram: K'an. The abyss. Water.

The Image

The image is that of people grouped around a center. It symbolizes water that is stored up in the earth in the same way that strength is stored up in the mass of the people. This is invisible in times of peace but always ready for use as a source of power in times of conflict.

Interpretation

A battle is ahead and you will need to maintain the confidence of those who depend on you. You are willing and able to take risks and to confront obstacles. Others are close at hand to help you and spiritual guidance is close by. Your situation is confusing and it will require care before it is corrected. You have to decide whether to fight against injustice or retreat. Avoid simply imposing your will on others. You have the capacity to lead but you need to develop leadership skills. It takes a lot of strength to capture the hearts of people and to awaken their enthusiasm. Use those whom you respect as role models. The idea is not to fight but to bring order to a situation and to protect others. Something significant will return to your life if you are open to it. Be firm and act righteously. War is a dangerous thing, so it should be used only as a last resort.

Lowest line

Don't let the rules get in the way of what needs to happen, but ensure that you don't lose all sight of the right way of doing things.

Second line up

Three events will show you that those above you will help you to change your life for the better.

Third line up

Rid yourself of old and useless ideas because hanging on to old baggage will bring misfortune.

Fourth line up

You have not made a mistake. Sometimes retreating is the right move to make.

Fifth line up

Be careful about what you say and don't try to get others to do your work.

Top line

Act on your ideas rather than adapting to those of others. You can achieve something significant at this time.

 **8. PI**

JOINING

Upper trigram: K'an. The abyss. Water.

Lower trigram: K'un. Receptivity. Earth.

The Image

The image of water and earth together signifies combining things of a different nature. The waters on the surface of the earth flow together wherever they can. This hexagram symbolizes those things that hold together and the laws of physics that make this so.

Interpretation

Honesty and sincerity will lead to success as long as you cooperate. By uniting with others you can complement and aid each other and you will discover the place where you belong.

Dishonesty will lead to misfortune. You may need to pull together in your job or in the family and to work for the good of those around you as well as for yourself. Get to the heart of the matter. Holding together calls for a leader. You should take on this role only if you are equal to the task. If you are not, then you can only make things worse. There will be a role for you whether or not you are at the center of things. Problems seem to come at you from all sides and you need to be organized. Relationships may dissolve as you discover new ways of putting things together. A new relationship with someone is possible.

Lowest line

Have confidence in your group and be sincere when establishing any relationship.

Second line up

Don't let connections slip away but ensure that you are with the right group of people. Guard against getting in with the wrong crowd.

Third line up

You are mixing with the wrong people. Be careful that you don't get hurt. There is no need to become intimate with everyone you meet.

Fourth line up

You are outside the group. Test your ideas and stick to your values. You have gained your position by your own efforts and through your own worth.

Fifth line up

Stop being predatory and give way to others at times. Sometimes you need to serve without seeking reward.

Top line

There is no central idea holding this group together, so you should leave before disaster strikes.

9. HSIAO CH'U

RESTRAINT AND SMALL ACCUMULATING

Upper trigram: Sun. Gentleness. Wind.

Lower trigram: Chien. Creativity. Heaven.

The Image

The image reflects the fertile soil of a river delta and the wind is blowing across the sky. A weak line in the fourth place holds the five strong lines in check. The wind restrains the clouds but is not strong enough to turn them to rain. A strong element is temporarily kept in check by a weak element, which implies that it is only through gentleness that a successful outcome can be achieved.

Interpretation

Conserve your energy and gather whatever you need for your plans to be successful. There are obstacles in the way, so you can only prepare at this time. Be patient, flexible, and tolerant; do what you can to make those around you comfortable. Times may be hard for a while, but if you are sensible you will achieve your aims. Restraint, sincerity, and empathy for others are needed. Friendly persuasion will be more successful than sweeping measures. If a relationship is failing it might be time to leave; letting go can be an act of love. You need to be determined yet gentle and adaptable.

Lowest line

Go back to the start and pursue your own course. Don't use force to get what you want.

Second line up

Something important returns to your life pulling you back to the past. Hang in there. If your path is blocked, wait for a better time before making a move.

Third line up

Trying to carry such a big load will make you irritable and argumentative. You and your loved one are trying to avoid true communication.

Fourth line up

Be sincere and try not to be irritable or angry. Avoid conflict. The truth will soon emerge, and that will exert more effect on the situation than the people or things that are creating obstacles.

Fifth line up

You don't have to act alone. Someone around you will offer resources that you can use, and they will help you.

Top line

Stay where you are for now. If you try to take control of the situation you will lose your direction. Success is secured a bit at a time, and caution will be needed before you can take action.

10. LU

TREADING

Upper trigram: Chien. Creativity. Heaven.

Lower trigram: Tui. Joy. Lake.

The Image

Heaven above and the lake below symbolize the difference between high and low, so this image refers to the right way to behave. Here the strong tread on the weak but the weak may make a stand, knowing that it will be accepted with good humor by the strong. The main concern is finding the right way to do things.

Interpretation

You need to think about how you can make your way in the world. Clarify what you want and what you feel your purpose to be. Wait for favorable conditions before acting. Be firm, even with yourself, and tread the straight and narrow path. Don't allow others to take advantage of you or slow you down. Remember that pleasant manners succeed even with irritable people. Use your intuition. Although there are difficulties, you can cope with them. Tread gently and plan carefully, then act with humility and caution.

Lowest line

Go your own way. You can make progress by using your own inner strength and by keeping things simple.

Second line up

You can smooth things over by continual effort. Stay hidden and work in the background.

Third line up

It is hard to see clearly. You cannot move freely right now so don't act recklessly.

Fourth line up

Be cautious. By going slowly you will achieve your purpose and overcome danger.

Fifth line up

Leave the old things behind and correct mistakes from the past. You can be successful only by being aware of the dangers ahead.

Top line

You need to examine your behavior and its consequences to judge what you can expect to happen next.

11. T'AI

HARMONY

Upper trigram: K'un. Receptivity. Earth.

Lower trigram: Chien. Creativity. Heaven.

The Image

The influences of heaven and earth meet and are in harmony so that all living things bloom and prosper. This also symbolizes a time of social harmony. The small and weak are about to take their departure, while the great, strong and good elements are coming on to the scene. This brings good fortune and success.

Interpretation

This will be a time of peace, harmony and joy, so you should share your happiness and good fortune with those who are less well off. You can plant for the future or harvest from the past. There will be good fortune, with progress and success. You can now develop your ideas and radically change the group that you associate with. Be firm and adaptable in your dealings. Those above you are willing to help when needed.

Lowest line

Changing the people you associate with and putting things in order will take you forward.

Second line up

You have a problem that only you can sort out and you may need to move away from certain relationships. You will gain credit for your actions.

Third line up

Difficult times come after peaceful times. Let go of something or someone that you care for and if it returns you will know where you stand.

Fourth line up

You may need to call on family and friends if you don't have the resources to cope with what is on your plate.

Fifth line up

Joining forces with someone younger helps to gratify your desires and fulfill your aims. Wait for the right moment to act.

Top line

Things feel as if they are collapsing and you need to call on support. This is not a time to test out new ideas.

12. P'I

STAGNATION

Upper trigram: Chien. Creativity. Heaven.

Lower trigram: K'un. Receptivity. Earth.

The Image

Heaven is retreating from you while the earth sinks lower, so this is a time of decline.

Interpretation

Poverty, losses and hard times surround you but a change in attitude or outlook will help. You have to accept that communications are cut off and that you are being blocked. Don't be discouraged. Good things can emerge from misfortune. Relationships are difficult now, so it is hard for you to know whom to trust or what to do. You are mixing with the wrong people. Be modest, withdraw and don't make a fuss. Imposing your ideas on others won't work. For the time being, your best bet is to ignore offers that place you in a prominent role and to keep your head below the parapet.

Lowest line

You need to associate with a different group of people. Follow what you believe in and be prepared to try out your own ideas.

Second line up

Adapt to what crosses your path despite the obstructions that bar your way. You are beginning to understand how to deal with your situation, but this will take time and patience.

Third line up

Don't take on anything heavy; you don't have the confidence or the skills for it yet. Right now, you can hardly cope with your current workload. Don't accept suspicious gifts.

Fourth line up

Deal with the things that obstruct you now. Happiness is at hand.

Fifth line up

Take a break, withdraw and let something go. Things are on the mend, so you don't need to worry so much.

Top line

What you thought was an obstacle turns out to be a cause for rejoicing. The bad times are over.

13. T'UNG JEN

COMMUNITY

Upper trigram: Chien. Creativity. Heaven.

Lower trigram: Li. Clinging. Flame.

The Image

Fire begins to rise to the heavens—it is the nature of fire to rise upward. Heaven moves in the same direction as fire, yet it is different from fire. Humanity needs to be organized into groups rather than being a jumble of individuals—there must be order within diversity. This hexagram symbolizes the act of friendship.

Interpretation

Teamwork is the key to success, although you may need to become leader of the team. There will be competitors and battles but there is light at the end of the tunnel. You will soon be able to make better progress and pass from obscurity to a brighter and more successful future. Find ways to unite people and goals that can be shared. Put your ideas to the test. Success is yours but you must share the benefits with others and work in concert with colleagues if you can.

Lowest line

You are about to join a specific group of people. Though this is beneficial, you should keep an eye on deals that are being done behind your back.

Second line up

Learn from the mistakes of others and think things over to ensure that you are seeing things clearly. Avoid getting involved with a group that has shady motives.

Third line up

Stop, consider and find help. You are facing a strong antagonist, so you may be unable to act for a while.

Fourth line up

No one can attack or control you and you are no longer boxed in. You can't fight, but you will see other ways around your problem.

Fifth line up

Having a cause unites people. Using sincere words brings the group together. Acknowledge your bond with another and remain true to your partner.

Top line

People are gathering but they have no sense of purpose. You can join in and hope that something good emerges.

14. TA YU

WEALTH

Upper trigram: Li. Clinging. Flame.

Lower trigram: Chien. Creativity. Heaven.

The Image

The fire in heaven above shines far and wide, so everything stands out in the light and become real and solid. Light pours over the earth and illuminates both good and evil. The two trigrams in this hexagram indicate that strength and clarity unite.

Interpretation

You will soon be successful but you may incur jealousy. Small losses may occur through not watching the pennies closely enough. Riches, wealth and success are ensured. An initial setback will be overcome and success will follow. Work and study will go together, and you will soon be in a better position to understand the tasks ahead of you. Don't go overboard trying to impress people but gently convert them to your ideas. Show respect for others and guard against becoming lazy and arrogant, otherwise you risk losing what you have. Grasp the basics and get on with the job quietly. Act wisely now and all will be well.

Lowest line

You may wonder if your hard work is worthwhile. You are laying a good foundation so nothing that you are doing is a waste of energy. Be aware of your problems so that you can work on them.

Second line up

You need a clear direction but you will cope with responsibility once you know where you are going. People will give you the help that you need.

Third line up

Concentrate on what you have achieved. Don't allow trivial matters to weigh on your mind. Be prepared to share what you have with others.

Fourth line up

Don't try to dominate the situation. Share what you have and allow others to shine. Avoid envy and the temptation to compete.

Fifth line up

You will meet people and you will impress them. Stay true to your ideas but don't be dogmatic or obstinate.

Top line

You have a winning idea, but when success comes do think of others as well as yourself.

15. CHIEN

MODESTY

Upper trigram: K'un. Receptivity. Earth.

Lower trigram: Ken. Keeping still. Mountain.

The Image

The wealth that is upon or that is inside the mountain is not visible. The path to your particular goal may seem long and winding, but it all comes clear once you reach your destination. Lowliness is a quality of the earth but in this case, the earth is placed above the mountain. This suggests that a modest attitude is best for the time being.

Interpretation

Avoid extremes and try to achieve a balance in your life. Keep things simple and stick to the facts. Be modest but not stupidly humble and don't allow yourself to become a victim. The best relationships are those that are on an equal footing. Sometimes you need to give way to others in order to restore the balance. You don't need to shout about your achievements because they will gain recognition anyway. Things are approaching completion. You have the power to shape your fate and to choose the kind of behavior that will bring success.

Lowest line

Think everything through twice and develop your sense of purpose. Your task will be easier if you get down to it now.

Second line up

Try out your ideas. By making a heartfelt statement you can get what you wish.

Third line up

Don't push yourself forward too much but carry on quietly. You will be criticized if you sing your own praises too loudly.

Fourth line up

Say what you think but don't argue or impose your will. On the other hand don't downplay your own worth.

Fifth line up

Take action. If you don't have sufficient resources, accept help from someone nearby. Do what is necessary.

Top line

Mobilize your forces. If you need something before you can proceed, now is the time to go out and get it.

16. YU

ENTHUSIASM

Upper trigram: Chen. Arousing. Thunder.

Lower trigram: K'un. Receptivity. Earth.

The Image

Electrical energy comes rushing forth and the thunderstorm refreshes nature. Tension is relaxed and there is a feeling of relief. You can expect joy and heartfelt enthusiasm.

Interpretation

Muster enthusiasm and prepare for a new project. You have plenty of energy. Ensure that all is in order and that there are no loose ends before you make a start. There are people who will help you. You will need to advertise yourself and to create an enthusiastic atmosphere, but don't fall for your own propaganda. Take opportunities as they arise and act with conviction, but make sure you do not appear over confident or arrogant. Consider the needs of others.

Lowest line

Create an enthusiastic atmosphere but don't leave others to do all the hard work. Don't boast.

Second line up

You are limiting yourself and you may be deluding yourself as well. Be firm, quit if you have to and don't allow illusions to mislead you.

Third line up

Don't be skeptical or doubtful. Don't procrastinate. Do what needs to be done and seize the moment.

Fourth line up

You can acquire what you want. Your sincerity and confidence draws others to you.

Fifth line up

You are confronting affliction, sickness or hatred. Keep calm and keep going. In a funny way the things that hold you back will do you a favor because they will stop you from rushing in and doing something stupid.

Top line

Let go of what is past. Although the situation isn't your fault, you don't have to let it continue.

17. SUI

FOLLOWING

Upper trigram: Tui. Joy. Lake.

Lower trigram: Chen. Arousing. Thunder.

The Image

Thunder in the middle of the lake serves as the image. It is a time of darkness and rest. Electricity withdraws into the earth again and rests. After being hard at work all day, you can allow yourself a good rest and recuperation.

Interpretation

Let go of what is past because a new focus is emerging. This is a good time for intimate relationships but not for business affairs. Having said this, it is possible to make new friends at this time. At work it is best to drift with the current and to allow others to show you the way or to take the initiative on your behalf. You will be in charge of your own affairs again soon enough. Adapt, be consistent, make progress and succeed.

Lowest line

Leave your dyed-in-the-wool opinions behind. You need to listen to others and to blend in.

Second line up

You may be taking responsibility for something that is not your problem or wasting energy on unworthy or thankless friends.

Third line up

Accept your responsibilities and you can get where you want to be. Avoid being led astray by silly people with frivolous ideas.

Fourth line up

The path you are following isn't going anywhere. You need to change your approach. People may try to take advantage of you.

Fifth line up

You are moving toward something worthwhile but you need to believe in yourself and in your goal.

Top line

You hold others together and they will call upon you for help. However, for the time being you can only follow. Right now, leadership is not for you.

18. KU

DECAY

Upper trigram: Ken. Keeping still. Mountain.

Lower trigram: Sun. Gentleness. Wind.

The Image

When the wind blows and bounces off the mountain. Then it blows down the mountain again and this double-whammy can spoil the crops and vegetation. This hexagram suggests that change and movement may be needed but won't be accomplished without a few hiccups. You need to avoid taking attitudes that could destroy what you are trying to achieve.

Interpretation

There is a choice to be made that could lead to success or failure. Losses, setbacks, and hardship surround you. Whatever is on your mind could lead to trouble so a change in attitude will help. Take time with your decisions, act carefully and avoid new commitments at this time. If you find the source of the problem, you can stop the rot, stabilize the situation, and bring some form of undeveloped potential into being. Even with care there is still some risk of failure. Something has gone wrong and it must be put right, and you may have to apologize for a mistake or sort out a misunderstanding. You need to be scrupulously honest in all your dealings. It will take some effort but you can make a new start on something now. You will soon be busy again. Avoid decisions on partnerships or marriage at this time.

Lowest line

Take advice in this difficult time and accept that some people in authority may be dishonest.

Second line up

Gentle consideration is called for. Don't hurt others by taking drastic action.

Third line up

If you bend over backward to adapt to a new situation you will regret it, so stick to your own ideas and finish what you have started.

Fourth line up

If you continue like this you will be end up confused and ashamed. Problems that have their roots in the past have to be dealt with.

Fifth line up

Use praise when handling others. You can gain status and authority and achieve your aim. Even if you cannot create a new beginning, you can obtain help to change things for the better.

Top line

Not everyone has to become involved in the affairs of the world, so it may be better for you to sit things out and to allow the world to go its own way for a while. You need to consider life and look inside yourself to see what is worthwhile.

19. LIN

GATHERING STRENGTH

Upper trigram: K'un. Receptivity. Earth.

Lower trigram: Tui. Joyous. Lake.

The Image

The earth is higher than the lake, which symbolizes the help that those who are in a high position can give to those beneath. The lake is immeasurably deep, so a wise person is also deep and he can pass wisdom on to others and he can guide them.

Interpretation

You need to deal kindly with those who are under your control. You will soon be in an excellent position, so be generous to others. Follow the advice you are offered if it is good, but remain firm in your convictions. Your troubles will ease and recognition and benefits will follow as long as you treat others kindly and with modesty. Problems are indicated later so your success may be short-lived, so the best thing is to enjoy it while it lasts. You need to work determinedly to make the best use of this time.

Lowest line

You are about to make an influential connection. Don't get carried away by what is happening right now but stick to what you know to be right.

Second line up

An influential person will help you. You don't need to worry about the future because you will soon see that your present difficulties are only temporary.

Third line up

You may be too easy going toward others. Be aware of your responsibilities but ensure that other people don't shirk theirs.

Fourth line up

Things are coming to a head, so this is the time to push for what you want.

Fifth line up

Those who know the score will help you to make the right decisions, but you must surround yourself with the right people.

Top line

You can expect a windfall and generosity from others. Don't sit around because this is a time to be active and to go out into the world. Those whom you teach and help will gain much from you.

20. KUAN

CONTEMPLATING

Upper trigram: Sun. Gentleness. Wind.

Lower trigram: K'un. Receptivity. Earth.

The Image

The wind blows far and wide over the face of the earth, so grass must bend to its power. Your mere existence and the impact of your personality can sway people to your way of seeing things. The wind blowing over the earth represents the kind of regular journeys that you need to make in order to obtain information that will help you to act effectively.

Interpretation

The immediate future will be difficult. You will feel as though you are being blown around by a powerful wind, so that you cannot achieve anything. The situation will improve but you need to be patient. This is not a good time in which to take action, because you need to look around for ideas and to gain more insight. Now is a good time to study or to begin training and to keep your eyes open for opportunities. You need to be aware of the wider issues. Things will change spontaneously. Don't take anything on trust but allow your intuition to be your guide.

Lowest line

Look around at the less obvious aspects of your situation and make concrete plans rather than just taking things as they come. Don't just think of yourself.

Second line up

If you are in a position of responsibility make sure that you are above reproach. You need to learn how to put yourself in another's place.

Third line up

Examine your life and decide whether or not to act. Pay attention to the effects that your actions have on the lives of those around you.

Fourth line up

Take advantage of your position, because you are now in a situation where you can use your influence.

Fifth line up

Think of others and don't act in a self-centered way.

Top line

Don't blame others even if they appear to be complete fools. You share some of the responsibility for what is currently going on.

21. SHIH HO

BITING THROUGH

Upper trigram: Li. Fire.

Lower trigram: Chen. Thunder.

The Image

Two powerful but opposing forces cause a massive buildup of power and a great noise. Eventually there will be a release because the storm will break and put the fire out.

Interpretation

Look inside yourself because a change of attitude might be just what you need. Perhaps you need a change of environment or you might need to leave behind familiar situations that have now become uncomfortable or unhappy. You may need to enforce the rules so that others start to behave properly. You can improve personal relationships by talking things over and by clearing up misunderstandings. Don't back off from a fight and don't stay put if things are not right and don't take things lying down any longer.

Lowest line

If you have strayed from the right path, you must recognize this and put things right.

Second line up

You will be faced with choices but the right one will soon become clear and this will help you to make the right decision.

Third line up

Your task may be hard but you must not give up. Someone in a powerful position is standing in your way, but as long as you persist you will get the job done regardless of opposition.

Fourth line up

You are not in a position of strength, so it will be extremely hard for you to transform the situation but you must do it anyway.

Fifth line up

Do what is right and be sure that others know you are being honest and decent.

Top line

If you have forgotten how to tell right from wrong, you will soon be shown the error of your ways.

22. PI

GRACE, ADORNING

Upper trigram: Ken. Keeping still. Mountain.

Lower trigram: Li. Clinging. Fire.

The Image

The light of the fire illuminates the mountain. This looks lovely but the light doesn't shine very far. Important questions cannot be resolved if they are based on how things appear rather than how they really are.

Interpretation

Be firm but also flexible and you will be lucky and happy. Dress well and look successful to sell an idea or promote yourself, and focus on the need to improve your appearance before attending an important event. Make everything look as good as possible but once you have achieved your aim, don't live beyond your means. Ensure that you are not looking at any person or situation through rose-colored spectacles.

Lowest line

Go your own way, be honest and avoid ostentation.

Second line up

Be brave and patient and bear in mind that things are not quite as they seem. If you judge things wrongly now you will suffer as a result.

Third line up

Things look good now so you may wish to sit back and not bother to keep on making an effort, but you mustn't give way to laziness, because you still need to persevere. One or two serious problems around you need to be dealt with.

Fourth line up

Things are changing but the new issues won't do you any harm. Make alliances and new friends. You may have to give up some comforts but the close friendship that is available will help you to find peace.

Fifth line up

Don't despair because things are not as bad as they seem. Your sincerity makes a difference. Be careful to make the right choice now or you may fall flat on your face.

Top line

Access whatever worthwhile characteristics you may have and rely on your good points. Your mistakes are not deliberate and you don't intend to hurt anyone so you will be forgiven.

23. PO

INSTABILITY

Upper trigram: Ken. Keeping still. Mountain.

Lower trigram: K'un. Receptivity. Earth.

The Image

The mountain rests on the earth. If it is steep and narrow and lacking a broad base it will eventually topple over. Like the mountain, you need a broad foundation to be secure. You need to be benevolent and generous like the earth that holds us all in place, because only then will you feel secure.

Interpretation

Losses and disappointments surround you. You need to lose outmoded ideas and remove those things from your life that are no longer useful. This is a poor time for speculation and business because backstabbing and gossiping abounds. Some aspect of your life is being destroyed so that you can build afresh for the future. Guard against people who might undermine you. This is the end of one cycle and it is a time to prepare for something new. You are not being cowardly if you don't do much at this awkward time.

Lowest line

People are trying to undermine you. You might do better by looking at things from another point of view. The situation isn't good and all you can do is wait.

Second line up

Set yourself apart from others and deal with the matter at hand. Be prepared to adapt. The worst is over and things will soon improve.

Third line up

Choose your friends carefully. You may have ties that are wrong for you.

Fourth line up

Don't do things the way that suits you right now, because you will hurt yourself and others. It would be better not to get too involved in other people's business.

Fifth line up

Opposing forces can unite for mutual benefit. Take the advice that's on offer to you.

Top line

Stay calm when things fall apart. Better times will come along soon.

24. FU

TURNING POINT

Upper trigram: K'un. Receptivity. Earth.

Lower trigram: Chen. Arousing. Thunder.

The Image

In winter the energy of life is still underground. Things are just beginning to move but the land must rest so that nothing grows or develops prematurely. You need to renew your energy by resting.

Interpretation

A change of season brings improvements and a renewal of energy, so be patient because improvements are on their way and everything is about to be reborn. Reunions are likely. Your current troubles, sadness and confusion will give way to improvements that are already happening even though you can't yet see them. Things have been delayed but the turning point will soon come.

Lowest line

Don't go too far away because you need to be able to get back quickly. If you can't do so, you could all too easily miss something important.

Second line up

Let go of what you are doing and be unselfish because the things that you gain will far outweigh any losses.

Third line up

You must face a ghost from your past and you will have to repeat the actions that you took before. You may not be able to reestablish a relationship because you may need to be on your own for a while.

Fourth line up

Get back to the center of things. If you return home, make sure that you come back on your own. You can manage alone if necessary. You need to take the plunge and get on with things now.

Fifth line up

Windfalls, benefits and generosity are coming and something new is on the way. You may have to return to some past destination. If someone challenges you, don't try to cover things up or offer trivial excuses; tell them the truth.

Top line

Retreat, reflect and start again. Find the right moment to return and avoid being obstinate.

25. WU WANG

INNOCENCE

Upper trigram: Chien. Creativity. Heaven.

Lower trigram: Chen. Arousing. Thunder.

The Image

In springtime when thunder rolls below the heavens, everything starts to grow. You must remember what it was like to be a child and perhaps return to a more innocent time.

Interpretation

Don't rush into anything without thinking about it. Be honest and stay within your own limitations. Be unselfish and straightforward, and don't let temporary setbacks upset you. Be ready for unexpected events and be flexible in the way that you handle them. Follow the directions given by someone you respect and good fortune will follow. Be spontaneous, and free yourself from obsessive ideas and emotions. If you don't look into things before you act, you will make mistakes through ignorance. Beware of getting caught up in other people's messes. Act as though you were an innocent child—that is, naturally, honorably and truthfully, without greed, ambition, unnecessary complications or desire.

Lowest line

Don't get entangled. Abandon the present situation and accept that it is at an end. Follow your intuition.

Second line up

This is not the right time to push for something. Just do what you have to do and don't worry about the outcome.

Third line up

The present problem is not yours and neither is it your fault, so don't get involved. You need to accommodate yourself to whatever is demanded of you. Trust your feelings.

Fourth line up

You can't lose what really belongs to you even if you throw it away. All you need to do is remain true to yourself.

Fifth line up

The mess that is surrounding you is not your fault. Let nature take its course. Things will soon change.

Top line

Keep your nose out of other people's business. This is not the right time to take action, so just wait quietly. You won't succeed by acting thoughtlessly.

26. TA CH'U

GREAT ACCUMULATING

Upper trigram: Ken. Keeping still. Mountain.

Lower trigram: Chien. Creativity. Heaven.

The Image

Heaven within the mountain points to hidden treasures. Some kind of treasure is hidden in the words and deeds of the past—perhaps some kind of legacy. Whatever it is, you can use it to your advantage. The riches of the past offer you something that you can apply to improve your current situation—even if this is something intangible like knowledge or a particular qualification.

Interpretation

You will shortly be able to make great advances in your career so put your ideas to the test and go after what you want. Hard work and steady progress will bring success. Difficulties will be overcome and even awkward people can be used to your advantage. You need to win people over rather than subdue those who oppose you. You can realize your hidden potential because you already have the inner strength and wisdom that you will need. Current obstacles will slip away but small ones will come into view. You may get involved in community activities at this time.

Lowest line

If someone offers you a challenge, turn it down and move away from what might become a disaster. Circumstances are holding you back now but the obstacles will soon disappear.

Second line up

Relationships have broken down. Don't try to compete with others. If you get to the heart of the problem you can resolve it.

Third line up

Accept that you have a period of boring work or drudgery ahead of you. Doing these jobs will free your mind and enable you to try out some new ideas. The main obstacle that lies in your path has been removed but you should guard against further problems.

Fourth line up

Gather your strength because soon you will have to carry heavy loads and confront difficult situations.

Fifth line up

An old enemy can't harm you. Stop relying on others. Now it's better to keep your thoughts to yourself or go about things in a roundabout way.

Top line

Don't envy others. If there is something you want, you can get it for yourself.

NOURISHMENT

Upper trigram: Ken. Keeping still. Mountain.

Lower trigram: Chen. Arousing. Thunder.

The Image

In spring the farmer prepares the fields for sowing. This is a time of preparation but also of tranquility. When you are peaceful, you don't say too much and rarely say the wrong thing. Tranquility helps you to develop a nicer nature.

Interpretation

You need to take in what has happened and to use your knowledge to dream up new ideas and projects. Nourish and encourage others and give some thought to your loved ones and help those who work for you. Beware of using people. Consider your words carefully. This is a time for rest and relaxation and building up your strength for the future.

Lowest line

Do what you have to do and don't envy others. If you show jealousy or resentment, others will sneer at you.

Second line up

You are short of something that you need but you can find it for yourself so don't ask others to prop you up.

Third line up

You are turning your back on something that will help you to grow and develop. Don't go in for short-term gratification but help others and give to charity.

Fourth line up

You are making an effort and it is working for you but you also need help from others.

Fifth line up

Reject stupid rules and regulations. Don't move around but stay where you are and test out your own ideas. You know your own shortcomings.

Top line

Now you can confront an angry ghost from your past. You need to deal with your responsibilities.

28. TA KUO

THE GREAT

Upper trigram: Tui. Joyous. Lake.

Lower trigram: Sun. Gentleness. Wind

The Image

A lake can overflow and appear to drown a forest but the trees stand firm and emerge undamaged after the flood has passed. You may need to turn away from the world for a while—almost if you too were temporarily under the water—but you will soon emerge with a smile on your face.

Interpretation

Taking on too much will stretch you to breaking point, so accept your limitations and work within them. You may be working too hard. Avoid jumping into something new because the current situation will soon improve. Don't be arrogant or aggressive, and don't be afraid to go it alone. This is a bad time to take up with a younger lover or rescue one who has problems, so however tempting this idea may be, you really would be better off alone for a while.

Lowest line

Prepare carefully, be clear about where you are going and concentrate on the essentials. This goal is worthwhile.

Second line up

Although your action may be unusual it will work out well. You may feel tired and in need of rest.

Third line up

You can't continue to prop up the current situation and the harder you try the worse it will get. You can still achieve a lot by accepting help from others.

Fourth line up

Take a break if you need to. Misusing your power will only land you in trouble, so don't be obstinate.

Fifth line up

Don't snub those who are in a lower position than you in favor of keeping in with those who are above you. You will lose out and cause some kind of instability.

Top line

Think carefully and choose the level at which you want to become involved. Something larger than obvious everyday matters is going on here.

29. K'AN

WATER, A RAVINE, DANGER

Upper trigram: K'an. The abyss. Water.

Lower trigram: K'an. The abyss. Water.

The Image

Water reaches its goal by continuous flowing and it fills up every depression in the ground before it flows on. Similarly you should strive to do the right thing all the time by design rather than by accident. Consistency is important.

Interpretation

There are some nasty pitfalls ahead and a warning of danger. If you must take a risk, then do so, but if you can leave things alone you would be doing yourself a favor. Conserve your energy because you will need it in order to face the dangers that lie ahead. Be careful and patient. Guard against theft, trickery and the misuse of alcohol. Women may have female problems at this time. Keep the lines of communication open and act according to your principles. When confronted with problems you must do the right thing, so only do what needs to be done and leave risky ventures for another time.

Lowest line

Avoid bad habits and don't do anything in a sloppy manner and don't accept sloppiness in yourself or others as the norm.

Second line up

Be flexible and look around for what you need. Calmly weigh what is necessary now and take things a step at a time.

Third line up

You won't achieve anything if you don't know what you want. Don't be misled into action but wait until the time is right.

Fourth line up

Act with sincerity and be prepared to go it alone. Begin with the things that you understand and the rest will become easier.

Fifth line up

Don't make a great fuss or overdo things. Stay out of harm's way and avoid being too ambitious.

Top line

If you go on like this you won't get anywhere. If you have been running with the wrong crowd or living a bad lifestyle you will suffer the consequences of your actions.

30. LI

CLINGING FIRE

Upper trigram: Li. Clinging. Flame.

Lower trigram: Li. Clinging. Flame.

The Image

Each of the two trigrams represents the sun during the course of a day. The bright sunlight allows you to see farther.

Interpretation

You are becoming more aware, so clear your mind and think logically and dispassionately about your life and your problems. Intellectual pursuits will succeed and a thoughtful approach to anything will be helpful. Passion may rule your head for a while, so you need to apply common sense. Recognizing your own limitations will help you to achieve success.

Lowest line

Be aware of the motives of others in order to avoid being misled or swept along. Act with reserve and composure.

Second line up

A reasonable attitude is necessary. Be clear in your own mind about what you want to happen.

Third line up

Don't dwell on the downside of the situation because the problem is only temporary. Don't overreact or waste time worrying about things.

Fourth lIne up

However good things are now, they may not stay that way because changes are inevitable.

Fifth line up

Grief at the end of this relationship may seem never ending, but there are benefits to be found even here. Try to maintain a balanced attitude.

Top line

Root out your bad habits and rid yourself of them. Something new is on the way.

31. HSIEN

RELATING, ATTRACTION

Upper trigram: Tui. Joyous. Lake.

Lower trigram: Ken. Keeping still. Mountain.

The Image

The image is of a mountain with a lake at its summit. The moisture from the lake irrigates the mountain. Be open to new ideas and don't become arrogant or opinionated, but be receptive to good advice in the same way that the mountain receives drops of water from the lake.

Interpretation

Attraction will bring people together and this could be the start of a blissful love affair or a successful business partnership. Try to discover why others attract you or what they want before becoming too involved with them. Be sensitive to their needs while still being yourself. A little flexibility now could open the door to a new relationship.

Lowest line

It may be difficult to see what you are supposed to be doing, but look around and see if you can work it out.

Second line up

Wait quietly until you need to act and then apply the right amount of effort at the right time.

Third line up

Stay where you are for the time being. Others will come along and show you what you should be doing. Watch your temper now because your moods are unpredictable.

Fourth line up

You are finding it difficult to make up your mind but if you think deeply you may be able to reach some kind of decision that you must then stick to. Avoid the temptation to manipulate others.

Fifth line up

This will be a good relationship, but you must keep your head and not get too carried away at the start.

Top line

Talking is one thing but only action will bring necessary changes. Take one step at a time and don't try to solve the whole problem at once.

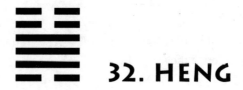

32. HENG

PERSEVERING

Upper trigram: Chen. Arousing. Thunder.

Lower trigram: Sun. Gentleness. Wind.

The Image

Thunder and wind are both mobile, so this hexagram represents change, movement and flexibility. You must keep abreast of the times and keep an eye on what is going on. Whether you stay as you are or go with the flow will be a matter of judgment.

Interpretation

Persevere and allow things to take their course because rushing ahead will bring problems. Don't insist on having things all your own way. A difficult situation will end and your relationship will strengthen with time. Let things happen in their own time.

Lowest line

If you want a situation to last, you have to think hard and put some work into it. Keep cool and take things slowly.

Second line up

Your regrets will soon be behind you. Apply the right amount of effort at the right time.

Third line up

Your moods are unpredictable and if you let them control your actions this will cause problems.

Fourth line up

Take what you need and slip quietly away without making a fuss.

Fifth line up

If something dishonest or deceitful is going on, cut yourself off from the situation in order to preserve your integrity.

Top line

Rushing at things will do more harm than good. Don't try to change everything overnight.

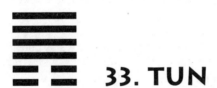

33. TUN

RETREAT

Upper trigram: Chien. Creativity. Heaven.

Lower trigram: Ken. Keeping still. Mountain.

The Image

The mountain rises upward, pushing against the lower reaches of heaven, but heaven retreats and remains out of touch. This symbolizes the way that you can retreat into your own thoughts.

Interpretation

The best course of action will be to withdraw in the face of conflict. This doesn't mean that you are running away from a situation but simply avoiding confrontation. It may be advisable to keep certain people at a distance for a while and you may have to step back before you can make a fresh move. Business is not good and you mustn't throw good money after bad. Don't embark on a relationship or anything new at this time. Conserve your energy and consolidate existing ventures with care. Avoid getting into a power struggle. Some people may seek to take advantage of you. Don't try to impose your ideas on others. When the right moment comes for you to take power into your own hands and make your move be sure that you don't miss the opportunity.

Lowest line

If you have retreated to a place of safety, stay put.

Second line up

Don't let anything pry you loose. Stay firm and don't give up the struggle, then you will reach your goal.

Third line up

You can't manage alone but it's hard to know whom you can rely on. Ensure that no one gets in your way or holds you back.

Fourth line up

By retreating, you can hold fast to your convictions. You are stuck in a tough situation.

Fifth line up

There is no doubt you are right but you should keep your opinions to yourself for a while and maintain a calm and friendly attitude.

Top line

Your doubts will disappear when your future path becomes clear. Depression and anger will fade when you can see your path.

34. TA CHUANG

GREAT POWER

Upper trigram: Chen. Arousing. Thunder.

Lower trigram: Chien. Creativity. Heaven.

The Image

The spring brings the first thunderstorms and these produce great power. This denotes that greatness depends on being in harmony with what is right, so you should avoid doing anything that is not in harmony with the established order.

Interpretation

This is a time of progress and others will follow your example, so act justly and wisely and follow your actions through to the end. Be prepared to take the initiative and make an effort to succeed but don't be forceful when it's unnecessary. Avoid throwing your weight around or being too one sided. If you have to use strong words be prepared to back them with action. Wait until the moment is right before you act.

Lowest line

You are tempted to force your way forward but this would lead to trouble, so reflect a while and don't act to quickly.

Second line up

Put your plan to the test and then persevere. Any remaining resistance will soon fade away.

Third line up

You don't need to use force and pushing too hard will bring trouble. Blowing your own trumpet won't do you any good at all.

Fourth line up

Just keep quietly plugging away and you will soon find that obstacles clear away.

Fifth line up

Changes are going on around you and these will offer new opportunities. Insisting on retaining the status quo or behaving in a stubborn or belligerent manner won't get you anywhere.

Top line

You have to deal with your responsibilities but stay within the parameters in which you find yourself. Some kind of deadlock makes it hard for you to advance or retreat.

35. CHIN

PROGRESS

Upper trigram: Li. Clinging. Flame.

Lower trigram: K'un. Receptivity. Earth.

The Image

The light of the sun rises above the earth spreading its rays over an ever-widening area. This shows that things are improving. Your nature is good but you may be behaving in a less than perfect manner due to the things that are going on around you. Center yourself and make sure that you are pure in heart. Be ready to give and receive.

Interpretation

Things are improving and you are on the way up, so this is an excellent time for success but you need to think of others as well as yourself. Communication is important and you should avoid acting aggressively. Take delight in what you already have without wanting more than is reasonable. People will rally round you and they will be willing to follow your lead.

Lowest line

Be generous and act independently. Do what you know is right and don't worry if others disagree or ostracize you.

Second line up

Accept the sorrow that this situation brings. Happiness will come to you. Take on responsibilities with compassion and intelligence.

Third line up

People have confidence in you, but you mustn't be underhanded if you want to keep it.

Fourth line up

Don't focus on obtaining money or possessions right now. If there is an obstacle to your progress it will soon disappear. If you need to start something new, you will also need to let go of something old.

Fifth line up

You won't regret acting now but you can't do much until you have removed one particular obstacle.

Top line

Use your strength carefully. You can't move forward just yet so don't charge into anything. Keep calm and have faith.

36. MING I

DARKENING OF THE LIGHT

Upper trigram: K'un. Receptivity. Earth.

Lower trigram: Li. Clinging. Flame.

The Image

In times of darkness you need to be cautious because you will upset others and make enemies if you behave in an inconsiderate manner. The flame brings the earth's darkness into the light, but you shouldn't shine your own light too brightly.

Interpretation

Don't be downhearted if things aren't going well, but be patient because things will improve. Be careful about whom you trust and act cautiously. Keep your opinions to yourself and try to not take on too much for a while. You need to play your cards close to your chest and keep secrets. Hide your disappointment until things change for the better.

Lowest line

You need to compromise or perhaps use a little force if necessary. Better times are coming.

Second line up

However much you are hurting, you should still put the needs of others above your own. You may soon take on extra responsibilities.

Third line up

Even if you have to remove someone abusive from your orbit, don't do this too quickly because some aspects of your situation are worth keeping. If something isn't working for you, drop it rather than persisting.

Fourth line up

You need to leave the scene of disaster before the storm breaks. There is no longer any hope of improvement.

Fifth line up

Hide your true abilities until things are clearer. You can't progress until the obstacle has been removed.

Top line

Persist until you can see the whole picture. You can't move forward yet, so keep calm and have faith in yourself.

37. CHIA JEN

FAMILY

Upper trigram: Sun. Gentleness. Wind.

Lower trigram: Li. Clinging. Flame.

The Image

A fire becomes fiercer when the wind blows and the effect of the wind becomes more obvious to those who are looking at the fire. If you have something to say, ensure that you make sense in the light of reality and present circumstances, and ensure that your words are backed up by your deeds.

Interpretation

You cannot do anything in isolation but only in coordination with close family and friends. What goes on in a household is a microcosm of what goes on in the world at large, so take note of how these mechanisms work. Behave morally, justly and with respect for others. In work situations, treat those who work under you as you would like to be treated. Give your superiors the deference they deserve because at this time it is best to stick to tradition and not try to buck the system.

Lowest line

Where all kinds of relationships are concerned, stay within the boundaries and stick to the rules.

Second line up

Do what needs to be done, avoid giving in to impulses and pushing too hard.

Third line up

You may have to keep others in line but try to strike a balance. It is better to be too severe rather than too weak.

Fourth line up

You need to balance what you give against what you receive. Follow the middle path.

Fifth line up

Act from the heart and show your affection. Stick to your values and you will achieve your goals.

Top line

Take responsibility willingly and ensure that everyone knows what he or she is supposed to be doing.

38. K'UEI

OPPOSITION

Upper trigram: Li. Clinging. Flame.

Lower trigram: Tui. Joyous. Lake.

The Image

Fire and water never mingle because even when they are in contact, they retain they their own natures. In the same way you can preserve your individuality while joining with others and you can avoid being dragged into dishonorable behavior.

Interpretation

Treat others generously if you need to turn conflict and suspicion into shared success. Work colleagues and family members may see things differently from you, but the differences are small and you may have more in common than you think. Try to be constructive and seek harmony. You are not always right so allow others some leeway, and even when you are right there is no need to harp on about it. Cooperate as much as you can and wait for this phase to pass. Being quiet and fitting in could be your best tactic for the time being.

Lowest line

Don't get entangled in the twisted emotions of others. You can't force people to like each other. Misunderstandings can cause confusion.

Second line up

By chance, you will meet someone who can help you. Working together will bring you good fortune.

Third line up

You can't get anywhere at the moment, and you will feel isolated.

Fourth line up

Although you feel alone, you meet someone whom you can trust completely. You will soon see a way through your problems.

Fifth line up

A sincere person will come along and help you to sort things out. You have no need to look back with regret.

Top line

Don't misjudge your friends or defend yourself against them. They have good intentions and when you realize this, things will be better.

39. CHIEN

OBSTRUCTION

Upper trigram: K'an. Abyss. Water.

Lower trigram: Ken. Keeping still. Mountain.

The Image

Water on the mountain represents the obstacles that you face. This is an image of a dangerous abyss lying before you and a steep, inaccessible mountain rising behind you, so it symbolizes how obstacles surround you. The mountain doesn't move so there is a chance that you can find some way around it and overcome the obstacles that stand in your way.

Interpretation

Difficulties surround you but these are part of an essential process, so try to find a way around your problem rather than moaning about it. Be constant in your objectives but don't apply force to achieve them because you need to be patient and think before acting. A direct approach may not be what you need, so try to look at things in a different way. Retreat and get help from others where you can. This is a particularly bad time for relationships. Keep going even when circumstances seem to be making it hard to reach your goal. In some way, a temporary obstruction may actually do you a favor because clearing it may make you stronger.

Lowest line

Difficulties are passing and praise is coming, but you still have to wait. Ask for help and you'll get it.

Second line up

Don't doubt yourself but act as straightforwardly as possible. You need to be single minded to succeed.

Third line up

You will soon have a reason to be happy. Ask for and accept help whenever you need it.

Fourth line up

You can't manage this situation single-handedly. You may have to abandon your present plans and seek a new way of doing things.

Fifth line up

You can't avoid your problem but help is available so take it and try to keep your fears under control.

Top line

You can't turn your back on the current situation but there is helpful advice on hand.

40. HSIEH

LIBERATION

Upper trigram: Chen. Arousing. Thunder.

Lower trigram: K'an. Abyss. Water.

The Image

A thunderstorm clears the air. You may need to put a few things right in order to calm the situation down. Mistakes happen but you shouldn't dwell on them because they disappear in the same way that the thunder dies away. You can forgive others in the same way that water washes everything clean.

Interpretation

Tensions are beginning to ease and you can make your way back to a more comfortable situation. The situation will come to a head and when it does you will know where you stand. Remember the lessons you have learned and avoid becoming a slave to the past. Show leadership at home and at work but allow others some leeway. Joining with others will help you to realize your ambitions. Leave unfinished business until you are up to dealing with it. Let things go and be ready to forgive others. Periods of sudden change can actually be liberating.

Lowest line

Don't complain about things because most of your problem is behind you. Tell your enemies to get lost.

Second line up

Test your ideas but make sure that you use the right methods. You need to rid yourself of your own bad habits.

Third line up

You are at fault and your carelessness might bring you trouble. Tell people who act like parasites to leave you alone.

Fourth line up

You may need to end partnerships and go it alone, otherwise the situation will get out of control.

Fifth line up

You may feel that there is no way out but you can find one, and when people see that you're in earnest they will stop pressuring you.

Top line

Someone is standing in your way and you must remove this obstacle.

41. SUN

DECREASE

Upper trigram: Ken. Keeping still. Mountain.

Lower trigram: Tui. Joyous. Lake.

The Image

The lake at the foot of the mountain evaporates a little until it is filled again by rainfall. The mountain represents the strength that can harden into anger but the lake is the symbol of gaiety, desire and passion. This suggests that there are times when anger should be curbed but also that there are times when you need to control your desires, passions and basic instincts.

Interpretation

Don't spend money unless you have to and hang on to your savings because an unexpected expense is on the way. You need to redistribute some of your money or goods for the benefit of others, and this could even mean having to pay a large tax bill! There is no need to be ashamed of poverty or shortages, because managing on less will allow you to appreciate a simpler lifestyle. Personal relationships may be boring, but avoid getting into something stupid for the sake of excitement. It's also important to curb your anger. In short, the message is to control yourself and avoid excesses of all kinds.

Lowest line

Finish things and leave quickly. Be ready to offer help where it is needed.

Second line up

Maintain your own dignity if you are to be of service to others. Know your faults and do something about them.

Third line up

A close bond is possible only between two people while a third brings jealousy.

Fourth line up

Behave nicely and you will soon get others on your side.

Fifth line up

Fate is ruling your life now so you are due for a bit of luck.

Top line

What you accomplish is to the benefit of everyone rather than just yourself, so improving your life will improve the lives of those who are around you.

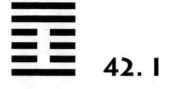

42. 1

INCREASE

Upper trigram: Sun. Gentleness. Wind.

Lower trigram: Chen. Arousing. Thunder.

The Image

Thunder and wind increase and strengthen one another, so this represents your ability to improve yourself and your life. When you see good in others you should imitate it and when you see faults in yourself, eradicate them.

Interpretation

This is a good time for increased activity and prosperity, so make the most of this period while it lasts. Some of your success is due to luck rather than ability. Be generous and don't seek unfair advantage over others. Business and finance are improving and close relationships are working well. You may have to make sacrifices for others. Their happiness and gratitude will make this worthwhile.

Lowest line

Use your extra energy to achieve something great. You may try to give others the impression that your motives are unselfish, but they are not as pure as you think they are.

Second line up

Fate is on your side and your actions can benefit those who are around you. Use this time to do something good for others with no thought of personal gain.

Third line up

Even things that look bad turn out well. Use your power and position wisely to ensure success.

Fourth line up

Don't hold back through selfishness. Someone else's misfortune brings you luck.

Fifth line up

True kindness and unselfishness on your part will soon be rewarded.

Top line

Neglecting your obligations to others will leave you alone and isolated. You are due for success so there is no need to be selfish.

43. KUAI

DETERMINATION

Upper trigram: Tui. Joyous. Lake.

Lower trigram: Chien. Creativity. Heaven.

The Image

When the water in a lake evaporates and rises up to heaven it can lead to a cloudburst. This image warns of the violent collapse that could happen when you don't consider others while amassing riches for yourself. As the rain disperses so must you be generous to others.

Interpretation

There is some kind of trouble around and you will have to enlist the help of others in order to counter it. You will gain more if you act fairly and are cautious; so don't allow bad behavior to destroy what you have achieved. Financial and career matters look good but it may be a good idea to take out insurance. There can be no compromise when it comes to removing evil from your life and the best way to combat this is to behave well. Love affairs are difficult and quarrels can spoil the atmosphere.

Lowest line

Use your energy to achieve something great. Don't shoot yourself in the foot by boasting.

Second line up

Be on guard and stay alert. By keeping your wits about you, you will be able to deal with whatever enters your life.

Third line up

Resolve to leave this situation and these people. You are pushing something further than it wishes to go.

Fourth line up

Don't believe all that people tell you but don't be too obstinate to listen to good advice. You may make others angry and resentful.

Fifth line up

You need to be firm and do not allow yourself to be deflected. If you need to kick someone, use both feet!

Top line

Communicate with others and try to avoid making a disastrous mistake.

44. KOU

ENCOUNTERING, TEMPTATION

Upper trigram: Chien. Creativity. Heaven.

Lower trigram: Sun. Gentleness. Wind.

The Image

The wind blows everywhere and it sets heaven in motion. Although it is daylight, a dark cloud drifts across to symbolize the way that you can be caught by temptation when you let down your guard.

Interpretation

This is a good time to flirt a little and enjoy your social life because serious commitments don't seem to be in the air just now. Business matters are likely to prosper but avoid being influenced by others in your work and social life. Guard against deceit, hidden agendas and your own ulterior motives causing problems. Calm persuasion will help you to influence others.

Lowest line

Find out what is holding you back or trapping you and remove it. Others may think you are snobbish even though you are not.

Second line up

Don't overspend or take on too much credit because a lack of available funds will make you look weak. Avoid confrontations.

Third line up

Don't let yourself be dragged into something that you feel is not right. There is nothing wrong with showing your feelings.

Fourth line up

Meet people halfway because you may need them later. If you reject them now and they vanish when you need them it will be your own fault.

Fifth line up

Be alert because both problems and opportunities surround you. There is no need to be stressed about bad fortune or to show off about good luck.

Top line

Don't let a minor problem become a major one. Keep your composure.

45. TS'UI

GATHERING

Upper trigram: Tui. Joyous. Lake.

Lower trigram: K'un. Receptivity. Earth.

The Image

If the water in the lake gathers until it rises above the earth, there is danger of a breakthrough. If you are prepared for problems to arise you can prevent them. Problems are more likely to occur when a lot of people are brought together. You need to be on guard against the unexpected.

Interpretation

You will soon meet someone who will be important to you, and this may be the lover of your dreams or a good business contact. At work, the best thing will be to create harmony and to encourage everybody concerned to make an effort because uniting for a common purpose will make great things happen. You need a sense of direction. Your sense of calm may be tested and you should be ready to act if things get out of control. Being with others gives you more power.

Lowest line

It takes a little effort to turn away stress and to trigger joy. You may be attracted to someone only to be rejected.

Second line up

Choose a strong leader to follow, as that will get you where you need to be.

Third line up

Work unselfishly for a cause. Although it can be hard to break into a group, someone will help you to do so.

Fourth line up

Trouble is on the way but that will soon be put right. Unselfish actions bring success.

Fifth line up

Your devotion to duty will gain people's confidence. Fate is bringing you a change for the better.

Top line

Your good intentions may be misunderstood. You may feel shy and awkward but you should join in.

46. SHENG

ADVANCING

Upper trigram: K'un. Receptivity. Earth.

Lower trigram: Sun. Gentleness. Wind.

The Image

The wind adapts itself to obstacles and it moves onward and upward without being stopped and without hurrying. If you keep going, you will do the same.

Interpretation

If you have done the groundwork in a situation, it will soon take off. Your efforts will be rewarded and creative enterprises will be successful. Avoid arrogance or overconfidence and be prepared to work hard to consolidate your gain. This growth won't continue forever because nothing does, but modesty and flexibility will carry you far.

Lowest line

Don't grab a plum job from selfish motives; just do the right thing and you will get there anyway.

Second line up

Keep your eye on the ball. Even if you feel that you don't fit in, your sincerity will elicit the right response.

Third line up

This isn't the time for doubts and misgivings, as these will only hold you back. Although things look good they may not last.

Fourth line up

Dedicate your energy to the good of the group. Find an original or unusual way of doing things.

Fifth line up

Don't let your successes go to your head but take things a step at a time and you will make calm, steady progress.

Top line

You are on the way up. But you still need to be conscientious and consistent.

47. K'UN

OPPRESSION

Upper trigram: Tui. Joyous. Lake.

Lower trigram: K'an. Abyss. Water.

The Image

When the water has flowed out, the lake will dry up and become
exhausted. This symbolizes the danger of taking the wrong path,
and it is a time when you need to remain true to yourself.

Interpretation

There will be hard times, probably through fate rather than your
own mistakes or stupidity. You may feel cut off from things and
need to gather your energy in order to reestablish communication. Don't run away from trouble but do look inward to find the
strength to cope. The losses that you suffer now may be necessary in order to show you what is truly important. Adversity
can sometimes be a good thing as it brings out abilities that you
didn't know you had. Guard against deceit and false flattery.

Lowest line

Don't allow past problems to color your future. A negative attitude will hamper your progress.

Second line up

You are bored and you need something new in your life. Be prepared and patient. Obstacles still need to be overcome before you get what you want.

Third line up

You are being indecisive and this will hold you back. Don't magnify small matters or deal with them recklessly.

Fourth line up

Help is slowly coming to you. You are very bored and may need a change in direction.

Fifth line up

You need something worthwhile to work for. Things slowly begin to take a turn for the better.

Top line

Don't dwell on failure or worse will follow. Pull yourself out of the pit of despair in which you have been wallowing.

48. CHING

THE WELL

Upper trigram: K'an. Abyss. Water.

Lower trigram: Sun. Gentleness. Wind.

The Image

The well benefits everything and everyone. Similarly, you can organize things so that all the separate parts cooperate for the benefit of the whole.

Interpretation

If you have to choose between people or between paths, use your intuition and keep away from those who are not straight and true. Dig deeply into yourself to find strength from within. Use knowledge that is based on experience to make sure that you stay on the right path. Things are good now, but you must keep a weather eye out for changes. Although you can change your address and start to move among a different group of people, you can't change your basic needs.

Lowest line

You can't move forward now but don't let fear overwhelm you. Stop wasting your life or others will lose interest in you.

Second line up

You may be stuck but you can ride the situation out. You are neglecting your own good qualities.

Third line up

You are unappreciated because you are not using your capabilities to the full. You can make small progress now so don't worry about the more distant future.

Fourth line up

This is a time of transition so don't be afraid to act alone. You are at the bottom, so the only way you can go is up.

Fifth line up

Use talents that you haven't bothered to exercise for some time past.

Top line

Get to the bottom of the situation but don't waste time over-analyzing. Get on with things and attend to practical matters.

49. KO

REVOLUTION

Upper trigram: Tui. Joyous. Lake.

Lower trigram: Li. Clinging. Flame.

The Image

The fire and lake can fight and destroy one other. Natural evolution means that you have to adjust to the changing demands of the times.

Interpretation

Changes are on the way and you may soon move or look for a new job. Divorce, marriage or even political changes may be in the air but these will bring good opportunities for you. Try not to be too materialistic. You need to reject old motives, settle old quarrels and act with sincerity. Your manner and presentation will improve and you will soon be able to impress others.

Lowest line

Don't make big changes; only small adjustments are needed now.

Second line up

You need to be fully prepared for the major changes that you make.

Third line up

Time your actions well so that you are neither too quick nor too slow. Avoid being selfish or narrow-minded.

Fourth line up

Focus on your goals; this is now a golden opportunity to reach them.

Fifth line up

Make a new start now because you have support.

Top line

Avoid impatience because you will succeed as long as you don't act impulsively.

50. TING

THE CAULDRON

Upper trigram: Li. Clinging. Flame.

Lower trigram: Sun. Gentleness. Wind.

The Image

Sun represents wood and wind while Li symbolizes flame. Together they stand for the flame kindled by wood and wind and this can suggest the idea of preparing food. The fate of a fire depends on the presence of the wood and similarly, fate lends power to our lives.

Interpretation

Ensure that your tools, equipment, and vehicles are in good working order. Look after your health; while this is a quiet time, you will soon need to move forward and you will need a solid base to move from. Be guarded, but don't worry about small mishaps.

Lowest line

Clearing an obstruction will bring you profit and insight. You will gain recognition for your accomplishments.

Second line up

Success will come as long as you don't throw your weight about.

Third line up

You are feeling unappreciated and ineffective. Tread water now and wait for better times.

Fourth line up

You are not using your talents properly. If someone supports you, treat him or her well rather than berating him or her.

Fifth line up

Follow through on your ideas. Others are jealous of your success but they aren't in a position to hurt you.

Top line

Success will be guaranteed as long as you are not too impulsive.

51. CHEN

TURMOIL

Upper trigram: Chen. Arousing. Thunder.

Lower trigram: Chen. Arousing. Thunder.

The Image

Thunder bursts forth from the earth causing fear and trembling; this symbolizes how we can be shocked into putting our lives in order.

Interpretation

Stormy weather lies ahead. You shouldn't panic but merely wait until it passes. Repeated shocks are stirring things up, and although you feel anxious, good things will come out of this period. Don't lose your concentration. What at first seems frightening will make you happy later. Be wary of problems caused by gossip. Incidentally, this is a good hexagram for anyone who communicates for a living.

Lowest line

There could be a shock on the way. You may feel at a disadvantage but this is only temporary.

Second line up

There are difficulties ahead. Don't pursue what you have already lost or throw good money after bad. You may need to withdraw for a while.

Third line up

Even though you may be shocked into immobility you still need to act. Your current situation is not doing you any favors.

Fourth line up

Avoid acting impulsively but be open to new ideas. This is not the time to take the lead or to be the leader.

Fifth line up

An upheaval can bring loss. Focus on the main issue and do what you can to put that right.

Top line

The bad times are ending and there is light at the end of the tunnel. Avoid bad alliances.

52. KEN

STILLNESS

Upper trigram: Ken. Keeping still. Mountain.

Lower trigram: Ken. Keeping still. Mountain.

The Image

Two mountains stand together. This symbolizes strength, stillness and calm.

Interpretation

Progress slowly along your present path and avoid unnecessary gambles or tackling tricky or difficult jobs. It's best to simply take things one day at a time. You may have to move through your life as if others weren't there but fortunately, peace, love and harmony can be expected at home. Avoid new partnerships and be true to existing ones.

Lowest line

Make your foundations firm as this will help you to build for the future. Your inner strength will help you now.

Second line up

You can't rescue others but you can center yourself. Listen to your inner voice.

Third line up

Don't repress your feelings or hide away from others. You can overcome your faults and failings now.

Fourth line up

Relax and meditate, reflect and retreat if necessary.

Fifth line up

Things are moving slowly, so go with the flow. Don't say something that you will later regret.

Top line

Be generous and kind to others and your plans will come to completion. Try to maintain an objective attitude.

53. CHIEN

GRADUAL ADVANCE

Upper trigram: Sun. Gentleness. Wind.

Lower trigram: Ken. Keeping still. Mountain.

The Image

A tree on a mountain develops slowly and then becomes firmly rooted, so this symbolizes slow growth. The tree on the mountain is visible from afar and its appearance becomes part of the

landscape. Such slow growth symbolizes the fact that it sometimes takes time for one's efforts to be recognized.

Interpretation

Happiness in love or marriage is ensured as long as you keep
to the rules and don't embark on a stupid affair. Other things
develop slowly even though there doesn't seem to be much
progress now. Don't make sudden changes but consolidate your
gains and allow life to take its course. You can achieve your goals
by advancing slowly and subtly, so work patiently and gradually
toward your objectives. Results will rest on a firm foundation,
so they should be able to withstand future storms. Plan well, be
honest and truthful and all will be well.

Lowest line

You must maintain the achievements you have made so far.
Delays and difficulties will actually help you to achieve success
because they prevent you from acting too quickly.

Second line up

You have made progress but now you need to guard against mistakes. You are ready to share your good fortune with others.

Third line up

Problems are facing you but you can cope. Avoid provoking arguments and all will be well.

Fourth line up

You will find a useful temporary solution. By yielding and serving
others you can adapt to the situation. Take time to relax and think.

Fifth line up

In the end nothing will hold you back but you shouldn't try to rush things. Friends will help you. Misunderstandings can be cleared away.

Top line

It is time for a fresh start. Take care to show affection to others.

54. KUEI MEI

THE MARRYING MAIDEN

Upper trigram: Chen. Arousing. Thunder.

Lower trigram: Tui. Joyous. Lake.

The Image

Thunder stirs the water in the lake and this creates shimmering waves. This suggests that relationships can take wrong turns that may lead to misunderstandings and disagreements. Keep your aims in sight rather than simply drifting along.

Interpretation

Be wary of getting into a situation that you can't get out of quickly, especially if this involves marriage or becoming entangled in an affair. Try to avoid situations at work and elsewhere where you are likely to be made the victim. New relationships are doomed to disaster, quarrels and heartbreak. If you can't get what you want, then at least try to want what you have. Give everything time because changes may suddenly occur. Even if they don't, you will know that you've given your situation its best shot. Love, sex and financial decisions are highlighted. Be sure that you are not seduced by something that is superficial or short term but look for truth and objectivity. Do not bite off more than you can chew.

Lowest line

Accept a secondary position cheerfully because it will lead to eventual success. Give value for money.

Second line up

Take an intelligent perspective. Being alone will offer you insight. Overcome your vanity and pride and avoid showing off.

Third line up

Have patience and sit this one out. Try to avoid making changes.

Fourth line up

Compose yourself and concentrate on what you want and wait for the right moment before acting.

Fifth line up

You are in the center of things. Value your ability to move and act independently because friends may let you down.

Top line

There is no advantage in clinging to this situation. If the only alternative is to take a low-level job then take it anyway. You can always move on to better things later.

55. FENG

ABUNDANCE

Upper trigram: Chen. Arousing. Thunder.

Lower trigram: Li. Clinging. Flame.

The Image

The combination of movement and flame brings clarity. This symbolizes that nothing good lasts forever and that what you have can dissolve or disappear.

Interpretation

You will be happy and troubles that come from outside will not harm you. Success, brilliance and prosperity are indicated, but there is a strong warning not to over-expand or overstep the mark. This is a good time to consolidate your gains but try not to lay money out on new ventures. Be generous to others. Cut through complications. Consolidate, put something aside for the future and prepare for any hard times that may follow.

Lowest line

Someone you admire can help and teach you. You may want more than you can have.

Second line up

Even if you know that you are right, others may not believe you. You can't solve the present problem so work around it.

Third line up

Your problems are passing away. If others don't appear to notice you, push yourself forward and make an impact.

Fourth line up

You can't win every battle but with a little help from your friends, you can win this one.

Fifth line up

A new chapter in your life will bring you praise and rewards. Friends may let you down and bring you disappointment.

Top line

Don't keep things to yourself but join forces with like-minded people. Trying to control others will alienate those who you are closest to.

56. LU

TRAVELING

Upper trigram: Li. Clinging. Flame.

Lower trigram: Ken. Keeping still. Mountain.

The Image

The mountain stands still, and above it a fire flares up and starts to float away from the solidity of the earth. This symbolizes separation from others.

Interpretation

This is a good time to travel on business or pleasure, perhaps even to run away from home! Get out and about and see what the world has to offer. You will need to market yourself, possibly while looking for a new job. Improve your manner and appearance and be careful to choose the right people to associate with. You may be outside the normal network and on a quest of your own. Be flexible and adapt to what crosses your path. Don't be afraid to act alone. Trying to reach your destination too quickly will fail, so move slowly. Concentrate on each step before progressing to the next one.

Lowest line

You may be behaving badly or being petty and if you go on like this you will lose what security you have. Don't make a drama out of everything.

Second line up

Take care of your property and avoid excess. Be prepared to relocate if necessary.

Third line up

Avoid being pulled into the conflict or you will be hurt. Be ready to move on and change direction.

Fourth line up

Being careless can be expensive. You may not enjoy holding yourself in check but you have no choice now.

Fifth line up

You receive praise from on high. Have confidence in yourself because now you can be successful.

Top line

Stop being self-righteous. Be strong and dignified, but don't put yourself down either.

57. SUN

PENETRATING

Upper trigram: Sun. Gentleness. Wind.

Lower trigram: Sun. Gentleness. Wind.

The Image

Sun is one of the eight doubled trigrams. It symbolizes wind and wood. It is associated with gentleness, so it is like a gentle breeze or a slowly growing and maturing tree.

Interpretation

You need to persevere and be reasonable so that others can accept your ideas. Bend with the wind and don't be argumentative. You can penetrate to the core of your problem by being supple and adaptable. You may need to be humble and to hide your virtues. Being steadfast will produce results. Have clear objectives and act honorably to achieve success but don't be pushy. Those who travel on business or who deal with people in foreign places will be successful.

Lowest line

Don't be indecisive but make decisions and follow them through. Knowing something is not the same as doing something.

Second line up

Get to the bottom of things and bring them out into the open. Evaluate and reevaluate.

Third line up

Don't make excessive demands of people. You can be successful so long as you keep working at it. Be decisive.

Fourth line up

All your regrets disappear. Think carefully and look before you leap. Combine modesty with action.

Fifth line up

Take some time to prepare and make sure that things are all in order. Unpleasant feelings may upset you.

Top line

You have gone too far in trying to correct things, so be firm but not too hard.

58. TUI

JOY

Upper trigram: Tui. Joyous. Lake.

Lower trigram: Tui. Joyous. Lake.

The Image

This hexagram is one of the eight double trigrams so it is an important one. It symbolizes the smiling lake and its attribute is joyousness. Two lakes are joined and they don't dry up as readily because one replenishes the other. This suggests that knowledge should be a refreshing and vitalizing force.

Interpretation

Your career and financial matters will be successful, especially if your work involves communicating with others. Careers that rely on talking, singing, acting, teaching or diplomacy will succeed. Express yourself openly and interact with others. Talk, bargain and exchange information. Inner contentment will be reflected outwardly to others and outer harmony will generate inner peace. Be humble and avoid arrogance and talking too much about your success. Your family life will improve and you will gain peace of mind.

Lowest line

Others seem to have control over your life just now. Be content with what you have.

Second line up

Trust your sense of purpose because other people will lead you into bad habits if you allow them to. Don't be drawn into activities that you believe to be wrong.

Third line up

An opportunity is coming but this is not the right one for you. Think before making a decision.

Fourth line up

Don't let your emotions affect your judgment. Self-indulgence and sensuality aren't everything.

Fifth line up

Strip away your old ideas and avoid being weak or manipulative. Recognizing danger is all that you need to protect yourself.

Top line

Things aren't entirely clear yet. Feel good about yourself but don't get a swelled head.

59. HUAN

DISPERSING

Upper trigram: Sun. Gentleness. Wind.

Lower trigram: K'an. Abyss. Water.

The Image

Wind blows over water and disperses it. This suggests that when something is stuck or jammed, gentleness dissolves the blockage.

Interpretation

There may be a move of house, a new business venture, a change of job or recovery from an illness on the way now. In some way you need to make a change in location. This is a great time to alter your attitudes and to improve your appearance. You can eliminate misunderstandings. A family may become scattered due to one or two of its members stretching their wings or moving on. Marriage and relationships will be put on the back burner for a while because you will be too busy traveling and working to concentrate on these matters. Follow a middle path and try not to stray far away from it if you wish to be successful. You may meet people from your past.

Lowest line

Avoid dangerous situations and deal with small problems before they become serious. If you have a good idea, act on it now.

Second line up

Don't rely so much on others but be fair in your opinion of them. An inspired idea will be useful.

Third line up

Don't allow desire for a love affair or for anything else that you shouldn't do distract you. Be an adjudicator or peacemaker.

Fourth line up

Ponder on what is truly significant for you. There is a large task ahead of you, so seek help if you need it.

Fifth line up

Your problems are all in your head, so don't rush around doing things to solve them. A good idea can pull everyone together.

Top line

Remove the possibility of conflict. If a quarrel is looming sort it out now.

60. CHIEH

LIMITATION

Upper trigram: K'an. Abyss. Water.

Lower trigram: Tui. Joyous. Lake.

The Image

A lake occupies a limited space, so when more water enters, it overflows. This shows that limits must be set. The image shows water below and water above, with the earth between them acting as a restriction.

Interpretation

The best approach is teamwork, so this is the right time to discuss your situation with others. You need to be cautious and to accept certain limitations. Reserves of energy, property or money will be needed while you sit out a difficult situation. When doors open again, you will be able to move forward, but for the time being you must follow the rules even if they are someone else's. Don't harm yourself or others with rules that are bitter or harsh. Limitations are troublesome but they can be useful. If we live economically in normal times, we are prepared for times of want. Stay calm, be wise and think ahead.

Lowest line

You have done your best and there isn't much more that you can do for the time being. Stop, remain quiet and don't step out of your familiar territory for a while.

Second line up

Don't let the opportunity for change slip through your fingers. You can't influence others now, so concentrate on changing yourself.

Third line up

If you are suffering, talk about this to others rather than bottling it up. Don't be dragged into other people's arguments.

Fourth line up

Say what you have to but do this quietly and without fuss. Concentrate on solving your current problems rather than worrying about the future.

Fifth line up

Say what you need to as nicely as possible and don't impose restrictions on others while ignoring them yourself. A split is inevitable.

Top line

Take action before everyone and everything falls apart. Avoid being too severe toward others or telling them how bitter you are.

61. CHUNG FU

INNER TRUTH

Upper trigram: Sun. Gentleness. Wind.

Lower trigram: Tui. Joyous. Lake.

The Image

The wind blows over the lake and stirs the water, making the invisible visible. It symbolizes a breakthrough in knowledge or understanding.

Interpretation

There will be great changes for the better in your career, business and financial affairs as well as in matters of the heart. A move is possible and a change of scene will be beneficial. There may be stormy weather ahead but this is probably due to the turmoil that upheavals of this magnitude are likely to bring. Think about legal actions before getting involved and put off serious judgments. Learn to be happy with yourself and your life even as you make plans. Material and practical issues will not be too successful right now but you will be able to find inner peace.

Lowest line

If you are always thinking of what someone else is doing, you will never be at ease. Get help if you need it.

Second line up

A new person comes into your life and shows you how to get exactly what you want. You are in charge of your destiny now.

Third line up

There is little that you can do yourself now, so take advice from someone in authority. Your strength lies in your relationships with others.

Fourth line up

You need to go your own way. There will be news that makes you happy or sad and the behavior of others can affect your mood. You aren't really in control.

Fifth line up

Your insight will be right and you will be able to act on your ideas. If others consider you a lightweight, show them that they are wrong.

Top line

Why go on like this? You need to concentrate on your good points rather than putting yourself down.

62. HSIAO KUO

MODERATION

Upper trigram: Chen. Arousing. Thunder.

Lower trigram: Ken. Keeping still. Mountain.

The Image

In the mountains, thunder seems much nearer than it does when on low ground. This can be quite frightening but there is no real need to be afraid.

Interpretation

Your progress will be halted and while this may be due to external forces, it could be due to your own feelings of negativity or fear. Don't waste your energy or get into a panic needlessly and don't let bad feelings stand in your way. There's no need to be a miser, so give generously of your time and resources and these will be repaid. Pay attention to detail because success will come in small ways. Do not be over ambitious but be modest and conscientious in order to achieve results. If storms arrive, stay safe and wait for them to pass.

Lowest line

You are overreaching yourself and you may act to your own detriment.

Second line up

Everything will go well. Be conscientious about fulfilling your responsibilities.

Third line up

You are in a perilous position, so be prepared to defend yourself. You may have to change location.

Fourth line up

You should soon meet the object of your desire. Don't try to stay in the same place now that your difficulties are passing. Your fate rests in the hands of others.

Fifth line up

Extremely good luck is on the way now. You need helpers around you to complete your tasks.

Top line

Rely on yourself but don't act selfishly. Aim only as high as you need to.

63. CHI CHI

COMPLETION

Upper trigram: K'an. Abyss. Water.

Lower trigram: Li. Clinging. Flame.

The Image

When water hangs over fire, this generates energy. If the water boils over, the fire is extinguished and its energy is lost, and if the heat is too great, the water evaporates into the air. This represents the idea that caution is needed to keep things in balance.

Interpretation

A cycle has ended. You should consolidate what you have achieved so far and you should guard against losing all that you have gained. This is not a time to make further changes but to sit back and wait until things settle down. Gather your energy and use it effectively. Act with caution. Marriage or a serious relationship is favorable. You have probably passed the courtship phase, so some kind of commitment is now required of you.

Lowest line

You are acting too quickly, so avoid stepping over the mark. Try to avoid reaching beyond your abilities.

Second line up

Don't chase what is gone but leave it to return of its own accord. You can succeed but you need help from others. Avoid drawing too much attention to yourself.

Third line up

Don't put up with difficulties or adapt to someone else's demands, even if you are weary and distressed. Keep your head down and get on with things. If you are plagued by negative thoughts replace them with positive ones.

Fourth line up

Be on your guard. Even if you know that you are right, don't shout about it.

Fifth line up

You need to be sincere. Keep your goals reasonable and take action on the things that really matter.

Top line

You are in too deep and you are not in a position to deal with this. Don't start anything new.

64. WEI CHI

BEFORE COMPLETION

Upper trigram: Li. Clinging. Flame.

Lower trigram: K'an. Abyss. Water.

The Image

The flames in a fire leap upward, while water flows down, so these two opposite concepts take two different directions. If you are trying to achieve something, start by investigating the nature of the forces in question and discover their proper place.

Interpretation

This is the start of a new phase but you still need to finish the projects that you have in hand. It may be necessary to revise your knowledge and to discard what you no longer need. Something new is due to come along, so rest and gather your energy for this decisive fresh move. The possibilities are great, so it is time to clear the decks so that you are ready for whatever comes. You are following the right path, but you must avoid disputes. Success will come to you in due course.

Lowest line

You are doing too much too soon and you don't really understand the situation. Celebrate, relax and enjoy your achievements.

Second line up

Start slowly and you will find that you can make it if you try. The time to act has not yet come, so you need to gather your strength.

Third line up

You are preparing for a decisive new move. A struggle is inevitable but you will overcome problems.

Fourth line up

Put your ideas to the test and change direction if you can. You have to confront your own fears and you might be frustrated for a while.

Fifth line up

Patience, determination, inner faith and focusing on your goals will get you where you want to be.

Top line

Get together with others and celebrate. Don't start anything new now. Relax and enjoy what you have achieved and leave the striving and yearning alone for a while.

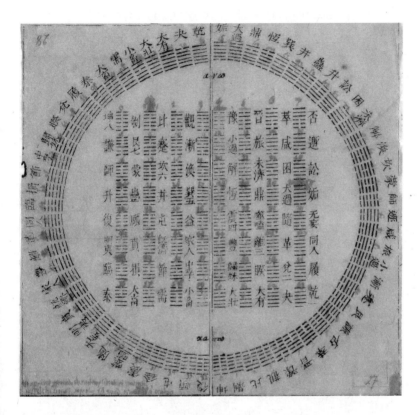

A 1701 diagram of I Ching hexagrams owned by German mathematician and philosopher Gottfried Wilhelm Leibniz. It was sent to Leibniz from the French Jesuit Joachim Bouvet. The Arabic numerals written on the diagram were added by Leibniz. From the Leibniz Archive, Niedersächsische Landesbibliothek

Quick
Interpretations

6

The I Ching is designed to be slow, meditative, and contemplative, but there are times when you need a quick answer.

If you don't have the time to delve into changing lines, trigrams, and hidden meanings—just read these quick interpretations.

1. Chien. Creativity. The King

Persist and make your efforts last because success is indicated. Decisive action brings good fortune, but you must do what's right.

2. K'un. Receptivity. The Queen

Take time to nourish the good things that are in your life and to bring new things into being. Perseverance helps you to succeed.

3. Chun. Difficulty at the Beginning

Finding the right location or the right kind of living and working space is the key to success. This will be a time of growth and release from tension.

4. Meng. Youth, Folly, Inexperience

Don't act yet because you are not ready and if you act rashly, your lack of experience will land you in hot water.

5. Hsu. Waiting

Wait for the right time before taking action. Eating and drinking with others will be pleasant or important in some way.

6. Sung. Conflict

Take advice from those who have more experience. Avoid arguments and conflict and avoid (or be prepared for) lawsuits.

7. Shih. Leadership

Show leadership and respect to those who rely on you and use your authority to ensure their obedience. There may be some kind of conflict going on inside your head.

8. Pi. Joining

Change the people whom you associate with and change the way in which you put things together. The timing of relationships is important now.

9. Hsiao Ch'u. Restraint, Small Accumulating

Accumulate small things that can be put together to make something great. This is a beneficial time to raise or care for children.

10. Lu. Treading

Find your way one step at a time and trust in the outcome. Pleasant manners lead to success.

11. T'ai. Harmony

Success is linked to tranquility. Be peaceful and flexible but be true to yourself. You will be protected by the spiritual connection between heaven and earth.

12. P'i. Stagnation

Don't be proud and arrogant for no good reason and don't get carried away with anything.

13. T'ung Jen. Community

All will be well if you act with honesty and flexibility and are cooperative and steadfast; harmonious relationships are indicated.

14. Ta Yu. Wealth

This is the time to succeed, so concentrate, be productive and share the results with others. Concentrate your mental and physical energy and use both now.

15. Chien. Modesty

Think and speak humbly in order to accomplish your goals because heaven rewards the humble now.

16. Yu. Enthusiasm

Prepare now for later enjoyment. Happiness and enthusiasm will carry you through.

17. Sui. Following

Go with the flow. If you want to lead others you must also know how to serve.

18. Ku. Decay

Find the source of the corruption. Interestingly, this hexagram actually warns about danger from putrefaction and poison, especially from venomous insects, although you may need to read this one figuratively rather than literally. If cleanliness or insects are a problem in your home or workplace, use some diluted bleach or an antibacterial cleaner and squirt some insect spray around the place!

19. Lin. Gathering Strength

Look forward with enthusiasm because good fortune is coming your way.

20. Kuan. Contemplating

Wait until you can see what is going on and then make appropriate decisions. Take a course of training; contemplate and meditate.

21. Shih Ho. Biting Through

Stress the positive achievements that you have made and don't allow others to stress the negative. Interference in your marriage or relationship will soon pass away.

22. Pi. Grace, Adorning

Beautify things and be brave. Beauty, adornment and embellishment are important in some way, so this might be a good time to spend some money on your home or your appearance.

23. Po. Instability

Strip away old ideas and habits and trim things down to the essentials.

24. Fu. Turning Point

Go back and visit some place from your past, but you must also welcome a new beginning. A change of seasons will bring a renewal of energy.

25. Wu Wang. Innocence

Disentangle yourself from difficulties and trust your intuition. A childlike innocence will help you more than trying to be clever.

26. Ta Ch'u. Great Accumulating

As in other ancient systems, owning and raising pasture animals symbolize abundance, and this is what is coming your way. Animals were considered a source of wealth in olden times, and for some they still are, so you can read this one figuratively or literally depending upon your lifestyle.

27. I. Nourishment

Accept what has already happened. Nourish and encourage others and consider your loved ones. Take some rest.

28. Ta Kuo. The Great

Gather your forces and don't be afraid to act alone. This hexagram is linked with new growth.

29. K'an. Water, a Ravine, Danger

Collect your forces and take a risk but avoid becoming trapped in a situation that is not to your advantage.

30. Li. Clinging Fire

Think logically and take an intellectual approach. Spread light and warmth among others.

31. Hsien. Relating, Attraction

This may mark the start of a love affair or a successful working partnership. This is a time of unity and cooperation.

32. Heng. Persevering

Carry on with what you are doing and renew your efforts. Don't insist on having things your own way.

33. Tun. Retreat

Retreat and be happy to stay in the background. This is not a good time for speculation or for business, so step back for a while.

34. Ta Chuang. Great Power

Have a firm sense of purpose and go forward. Focus your mind and your energies and take the initiative.

35. Chin. Progress

Be ready to give and receive. Your fortunes are improving but you must avoid aggression.

36. Ming I. Darkening of the Light

Hide your light under a bushel for a while and accept that there will be difficulties. Be cautious and restrained but don't allow misery to grind you down.

37. Chia Jen. Family

Households and family life are what will count now, so stick together with your loved ones and look after them.

38. K'uei. Opposition

Be aware of what's going on. Turn conflict into creative tension. Don't force your opinions down the throats of others but allow them to have their own ideas.

39. Chien. Obstruction

Rethink the situation. This is a poor time for everything and love relationships seem to be especially badly starred.

40. Hsieh. Liberation

Solve your problems by untying the knots that bind you. If something or someone is weighing you down or if something is no longer working, let it go.

41. Sun. Decrease

Mist below mountains means that you can't see where you are going. If you are doing too much or if you are involved in too many things, let something go.

42. I. Increase

Expand what you do during this fertile time. Abundance and wealth are in store for you.

43. Kuai. Determination

Make a decision and act with resolution. The outlook for money and business is good, but it would be worth taking out insurance.

44. Kou. Encountering, Temptation

Welcome what is happening but be prepared to let go of things that are no longer useful to you. Relationships, love, sex and unions of all kinds will make you happy.

45. Ts'ui. Gathering

A great effort brings great rewards. You will soon meet someone who will be important to you.

46. Sheng. Advancing

Make an effort and move forward step by step. If you have done the groundwork, a project will take off.

47. K'un. Oppression

Look within yourself to find the way to break free. Adverse times are character building, so don't run away from trouble.

48. Ching. The Well

Communicate and network with others. If you need to make tough choices, pray to your gods and use your intuition.

49. Ko. Revolution

Strip away the old. Shed old ideas like a snake sheds its skin.

50. Ting. The Cauldron, Holding

Hold on and transform your problem. Ensure that your tools, equipment, mode of transport, etc., are in good working order.

51. Chen. Turmoil

Stormy weather is ahead but don't panic. You will soon deal with new things that might be hard to cope with for a while or until you get used to them.

52. Ken. Stillness

Keep calm. Don't take unnecessary gambles or take on more jobs than you can cope with. Peace and love can be expected in the home.

53. Chien. Gradual Advance

Go slowly and advance at the same speed as a tortoise would. This is a good time for love and marriage.

54. Kuei Mei. The Marrying Maiden

If you are being victimized or badly treated, stay put for the time being because it looks as though things will change of their own accord. Realize your hidden potential.

55. Feng. Abundance

Prosperity and happiness are around you, but you must not over-spend or overexpand. Give to others but don't leave yourself short.

56. Lu. Traveling

You may feel as though you are on the outside of a situation looking in, or you may leave a certain place or situation in order to look into other ideas or solutions to your problems. Travelling and journeys, especially solitary journeys, are fortunate. Expect to spend time alone.

57. Sun. Penetrating

Gently penetrate to the heart of the problem. The energy of trees and plants that can bend with the wind might inspire you.

58. Tui. Joy

Express yourself and join others in a variety of enterprises. Family life will soon be good. You will have peace of mind.

59. Huan. Dispersing

A change of location is on the way and you may leave loved ones or colleagues behind for a while. Clear away whatever is blocking you or clouding the light.

60. Chieh. Limitation

Teamwork and going by other people's rules will help you now. Keep your opinions to yourself. When the time is right, you will be able to take charge of the situation once again.

61. Chung Fu. Inner Truth

Be true to yourself and others and you will gain their trust. Connect your inner and outer life. Career, business, money and love are all looking good now. A move is possible.

62. Hsiao Kuo. Moderation

Progress will be halted but don't allow worry or negativity to get you down. Carefully adapt to each of the situations that surround you.

63. Chi Chi. Completion

A cycle has already ended and the situation is already changing. Don't act yet but allow things to settle down. Guard against losing what you have gained. Marriage and love are successful at this time.

64. Wei Chi. Before Completion

The previous hexagram is called completion, but this one says before completion. This suggests that you need to tie up loose ends before moving on to something else, so gather your energy for a decisive new move.

Fu Hsi observes the turtle emerge from the water, with the original trigrams etched on it shell. Song dynasty, 11th century. In the collection of the National Palace Museum.

Other Titles in the *Plain & Simple* Series

Hampton Roads Publishing Company

...for the evolving human spirit

Hampton Roads Publishing Company publishes books on
a variety of subjects, including spirituality, health,
and other related topics.
For a copy of our latest catalog, call (978) 465-0504 or visit our
distributor's website at *www.redwheelweiser.com*. You can also sign
up for our newsletter and special offers by going to
www.redwheelweiser.com/newsletter